Anglo - American Culture

Variously Written, Compiled and Edited By

Ben Garrido and Young-Joo Jeon

Shinasa

User's Guide

Thank you for choosing our textbook on Anglo-American culture. This book seeks to explore fundamental differences between Korean and Anglo-American traditions with a series of historical narratives. We want to stress, from the beginning, that this is not intended as a history book. Indeed, it is intended as a tool to help Korean students critically question their own cultural assumptions while also learning to empathize with Western beliefs, fears and resentments. As such, students should stress the conceptual and narrative elements of each chapter, rather than memorizing dates or names. Indeed, the study questions included at the end of each chapter are specifically designed to encourage subjective and open-ended answers.

We chose to emphasize the differences between Anglo-American and Korean culture because, we believe, a failure to understand or empathize with dramatically different cultural traditions sets students up for a lifetime of culture shock and anxiety in the presence of Westerners. A morally balanced, nuanced understanding of Anglo-American culture, on the other hand, will give students the confidence and knowledge base necessary to facilitate smooth cross-cultural communication.

We've chosen two main threads and an important tangent as our framing devices in this book. The first thread concerns the treatment of outsiders. While Korea has, historically, worked to protect its traditions and keep foreign elements out, England and America have been uniquely shaped by the nearly two thousand year-old fight between those who want to open doors to foreigners and those who'd prefer to huddle down in their native cultures. We explore this thread in various ways – the Roman conquest of Britain and its associated wave of intermarriage and immigration, William Penn's "last, delightful asylum" for American Indians, Andrew Jackson's purges to preserve the white race, Cecil Rhodes' plan to out-breed the "lesser races," Malcolm X struggling to decide if white and black can coexist and even the debate of whether terrorism should close American doors to the world at large.

The second thread concerns the thousand year-old struggle between those who wish to concentrate power in a central city, person or government and those who wish for local control. This hasn't really been a problem in Korea, where most citizens are content to let Seoul call the shots. However, the struggle between local and central control has shaped Anglo-American culture in ways difficult for Korean students to understand. We explore this issue via narratives on William the Conqueror's devastating yet modernizing centralization of Britain, the Magna Carta's attempt to both tame central authority and ensure national cohesion, Robert E. Lee's agonizing decision to choose his state over his country and the – by Korean standards – singularly unusual phenomenon of Libertarianism in America.

Finally, we've included two chapters focusing on what it means to be a man or woman in the Anglo-American cultural sphere. We've chosen Queen Elizabeth I as an ideal for Western women and Theodore Roosevelt as a representative of manliness.

At all points in this book, students will be asked to compare the historical characters and movements of England and America with the historical characters and movements in their native culture. We sincerely hope this creates not a consensus around dry facts, but the seeds of a vibrant, diverse harvest of opinion and insight.

Sincerely,
Ben Garrido, Professor, Mokwon University
Young-Joo Jeon, Professor, Mokwon University

이 책을 사용하시는 분들께

영미권 문화에 대한 본 교재를 선택해주셔서 감사합니다. 이 책은 역사적 사례를 통해 한국 문화와 영미권 문화의 전통에서 나오는 근본적인 차이점을 탐구하고자 합니다. 먼저 이 책은 역사서적이 아님을 강조하고 싶습니다. 오히려 본 책을 통해 한국 학생들이 자신들의 문화에 관한 추정적 사실들을 비판적으로 되돌아보고 서양문화에 대한 신념, 두려움, 그리고 객관적 사실에 대한 이해를 중심으로 학습하기 바라는 바입니다. 따라서, 학생들은 이 책에 나오는 이름과 날짜 등을 기억하는 것보다 각 장의 개념과 이야기 요소를 더 중요하게 생각하며 학습할 필요가 있습니다. 실제로, 각 장의 끝부분에 포함된 학습을 위한 질문은 지극히 주관적이고 개방적인 답변을 유도하기 위한 것입니다.

우리가 영미권 문화와 한국문화의 차이점을 강조하기로 한 이유는 전혀 다른 두 문화에 관한 한국학생들의 이해 부족 또는 공감대 형성의 실패가 자칫 평생 갈 수 있는 문화적 충격과 영·미문화에 대한 오해를 유발할 수 있다는 점에서 출발했습니다. 영미문화의 도덕적 균형 및 미묘한 차이의 이해, 다른 문화권 사람들과 소통하는 데 있어 용이한 자신감과 지식을 이 책을 통해 전달하고자 하는 바입니다.

우리는 이 책에서 주된 두 가지 이야기와 더불어 중요한 접선을 구성요소로 하였습니다. 첫 번째 이야기는 외부인에 대한 태도입니다. 역사적으로 한국은 전통을 지키고 외국문화를 배척하려는 노력이 있었던 반면, 영국과 미국의 문화는 대략 2000년간 외부문화에 개방적인 사람들과 그렇지 않은 사람들 사이의 갈등이 만들어 낸 특별한 산물이라고 할 수 있습니다. 우리는 이러한 이야기를 풀어 나갈 때 다양한 방법으로 접근할 것입니다 - 로마의 영국정복과 그에 따른 결혼과 이민, 윌리엄 펜William Penn의 미국 원주민을 위한 "마지막으로 기분 좋은 망명", 앤드류 잭슨Andrew Jackson의 백인 인종 보호를 위한 숙청, 세실로즈Cecil Rhodes의 "열등한 인종" 배척 계획, 말콤 X의 백인과 흑인이 한 사회에서 공존할 수 있는지에 대한 결정의 어려움 그리고 미국이 테러와의 전쟁이라는 이유로 세계에 대해 미국이 보수적이어야 하는지에 대한 논쟁 등을 일부 다룰 것입니다.

두 번째 이야기는 중심이 되는 도시, 개인, 또는 정부에 권력을 집중시키려는 집단과 지방에 권력을 분산시키려는 집단의 대략 1000년이 된 투쟁에 관한 것입니다. 이러한 권력 문제는 서울이 중심으로 이루어지는 권력체계에 대체적으로 동의하는 한국사회에서는 찾아보기 힘든 예입니다. 그래서 지역 세력과 중앙권력 체계의 갈등으로 빚어진 영미권 문화는 한국 학생들에게 이해하기 힘든 주제가 될 수도 있습니다. 억압적이였지만 현대화를 이끌어 낸 윌리엄 1세William the Conqueror의 영국의 중앙집권화, 마그나카르트타Magna Carta의 중앙권력 지배적인 사회기반 구축과 국가 화합 시도, 조국보다 자신의 주(州)를 선택한 로버트 E.리Robert E. Lee의 이러한 결정은 한국 사회의 기준으로 봤을 때 미국 자유주의의 독단적이고 특이한 현상으로 정의할 수 있습니다.

마지막으로, 우리는 영미 문화권에서 남자 또는 여자로 살아가는 것이 무엇을 의미하는지에 관해 초점을 맞춘 챕터를 포함시켰습니다. 우리는 남성다움의 대표로 미국의 32대 대통령 테오도어 루스벨트를 선정했고, 이상적인 서구권 여성 대표로 영국의 엘리자베스 여왕 1세를 선택했습니다.

이 책의 많은 영역에서 학생들은 한국 자문화권의 역사적 주요 인물과 사회적 운동을 영미권 문화에서 존재했던 그것들과 비교하면서 학습하게 될 것입니다. 우리는 이 책을 통해서 학생들이 특정 사실에 관한 의견을 형성하기보다 다양한 분야에서의 의견과 통찰력을 기를 수 있는 기회가 되길 바랍니다.

목원대학교 사범대학 영어교육과
교수 벤가리도
교수 전영주

CONTENTS

01

Basic Information about the United States

Pre-reading vocabulary and phrases

revolt	an act of trying to change a government, often using violence
protestant	a member of one of the Christian Churches that separated from the Roman Catholic Church during the 16th century
inclusive	trying to include many different types of people
legislature	the group of people in a country or part of a country who have the power to make and change laws
heritage	belonging to the culture of a particular society such as traditions, languages or buildings, that were created in the past and still have historical importance
poverty	the state of being very poor

The United States came into existence on July 4th, 1776. On that day, 56 representatives of 13 states, all of them white men, signed a letter to George III, King of England. They said they were going to revolt and make a new country.

Those representatives said that every man is created equal. They said this because they wanted to tell the English "hey, we're people too." They were angry that the king didn't listen to them, they were angry they had no control of the English government. They wanted respect.*

However, the representatives had many different ideas about what "equal" meant, and they had many different ideas what "man" meant. A couple of them thought "equal man" meant all human beings. A few more thought "equal man" meant "only males from Western European families." Most thought "equal man" meant "only males, only Christians, only Protestants and only people from English families, and only if they own land."

As time has passed, "equal man" got more and more meanings. In the early 1800's, white men without land became "equal men." Then, in some areas, Eastern Europeans, Native Americans and former slaves became "equal men." Catholics, Muslims, Jews and Buddhists became "equal men" a little after that. Women became "equal men" in the early 20th century. In modern times, homosexuals have nearly completed their struggles to become "equal men."

Those representatives in 1776 told King George that all men have rights. All men have the right to life, all men have the right to freedom and all men have the right to chase happiness. But again, they meant different things. Most of them owned slaves, who certainly did not have the right to freedom, happiness or even life.

They generally weren't talking about women, who were expected to obey their husbands. They weren't talking about Native Americans because they didn't think the Native Americans were real humans. And like "equal men," the meaning of "rights" has changed over time, becoming more and more inclusive.

Group Activity: With your friends, discuss who you think are most likely to become the next "equal men" in your country. Are there any groups of people you think shouldn't be "equal men?"

The representatives wanted King George to know that they were building a new country, free from English domination, but they couldn't agree on what "country" meant. Those from the North generally thought a new country would have power located in the capital city. They imagined something close to the modern South Korean government, with a strong President working with a strong legislature and a strong judicial system. They thought a strong central government would make their country powerful and efficient.

Those from the South generally believed a strong government would take their freedoms. According to their "states' rights" theory*, they wanted each state to act like its own country. They thought the president should be weak, they wanted the capital city to be weak. The United States, they thought, should be more like the EU – a group of friendly but independent countries. 86 years after those representatives met, their ancestors would kill more than half a million Americans because of this exact disagreement.

Americans disagreeing about the size of the central government.

Some of those representatives dreamt of the great Western territories. Calling their ideology "Manifest Destiny,"* they imagined taking the land away from the Native Americans and giving it to farmers, factory owners and explorers. They thought Americans should be tough, independent and free. Their ideas live on today in cowboy movies and the small country towns where most Western Americans live. Tough, independent Westerners found gold in Nevada and made thousands of poor immigrants into rich factory owners in California, Oregon and Washington. The Western mindset created thousands of people who, even today, build their own houses, fix their own cars and kill their own food. The West became the home of people who don't need help from anybody else.

Some of the representatives dreamt of the South. They thought of long, slow days in the sun. They imagined a land of gentle manners and strong traditions. They wanted people to understand their heritage and protect the old beliefs. Even today, when older Americans retire, they often go south. In the South, they can escape change, they can get away from having to deal with a new problem every day. In the South, good families make good people, bad families make bad people and there's no need to worry about that changing.

Some of the representatives dreamt about huge cities and great industry. They imagined bending nature to their desires. They imagined new technologies, stronger societies and new ways of thinking. They wanted New York to be a little bit better, a little bit faster and a little bit bigger every day. These people built the great railroads connecting California and New York. They created banks and great universities like Harvard and Yale. They burned traditions to the ground and built new empires on the ashes. Even today, when a revolutionary idea emerges, it's probably coming from the North. Even today, when a young person wants to change the world, he or she goes north.

Group Activity: The West is known for independence and toughness. The North is famous for business and industry. The South is famous for traditions. How are these places similar to and different from Korean provinces?

These representatives in 1776 created a country that would come to have 50 states and 330,000,000 citizens. Their country would grow to 9,857,000 square kilometers - 98 times larger than South Korea. Their country would accept millions of immigrants from Italy, Russia, Greece, Germany, France, Ireland, Africa, Mexico and China. Their descendants would speak English, Spanish and Polish; Korean, Vietnamese and Arabic. Their descendants would create a country of overwhelming military and economic power, but they would also create a country with crime problems and far too much poverty. Indeed, according to Business Insider, US murder rates are two to three times higher in the US than in Canada, Britain or Spain.* According to the Economic Policy Institute, the childhood poverty rate was by far the worst in the OECD.*

Their culture would dominate the world for both good and bad. America would give the world both Hollywood movies and atomic bombs, dozens of new democracies and the drug trade, a rebuilt Europe and a devastated South America. Coca Cola, Apple, Levi Strauss, the Ford Motor Company, J.P. Morgan, Microsoft, McDonald's, FUBU, General Electric, Starbucks – all of these companies emerged from an America both devoted to innovation and willing to crush competitors.

Trying to understand the modern Western world without understanding the United States is like trying to understand Asia without understanding China.

From left - John Pemberton, inventor of Coca Cola, Sergey Brin, co-founder of Google, Draymond John, founder of FUBU

Resources	
For a full copy of the Declaration of Independence, with Korean translation, visit www.happycampus.com/doc/4545851	
For an explanation of states' rights theory, visit http://legal-dictionary.thefreedictionary.com/States%27+rights+doctrine	
For more information about Manifest Destiny, visit http://www.history.com/topics/manifest-destiny	
For more information about murder rates, visit www.businessinsider.com/us-vs-western-homicide-rates-2014-11	
For more information about poverty, visit http://www.epi.org/publication/ib339-us-poverty-higher-safety-net-weaker/	

#1

Positive Effects of US Culture.	Negative Effects of US Culture.
1.	1.
2.	2.
3.	3.
4.	4.
5.	5.

#2

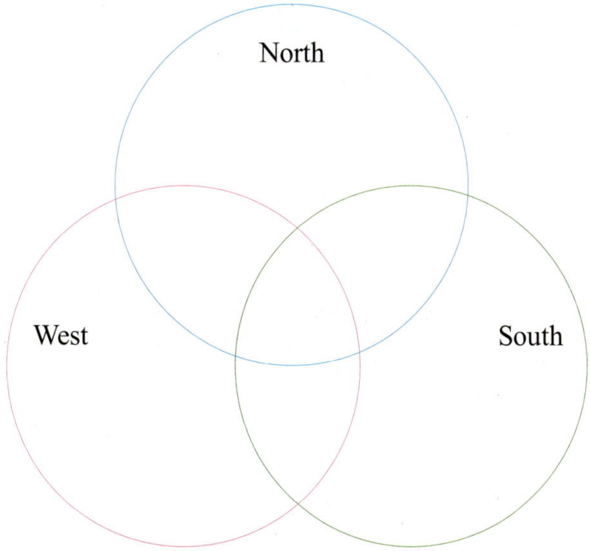

#3

Essay: Which part of the US would you most like to live in and why?

02

Basic Information about Great Britain

Pre-reading vocabulary and phrases

illiterate	not able to read or write
conquestt	the act of taking control of a country
imperialism	a system in which a country rules other countries, sometimes having used force to get power over them
globalization	the increase of trade around the world, especially by large companies producing and trading goods in many different countries
vaccination	to give someone a substance to stop them from getting a disease
opium	a drug made from the seeds of a poppy flower

Just as you cannot understand the modern West without understanding the US, you cannot understand the US without understanding Britain. A large island off the northwest coast of Europe, Great Britain is very old culturally, amazingly young as a nation and has been extremely influential in the world. At its height in the 19th century, Great Britain controlled the largest empire in the history of earth.

The British Isles have had civilization for more than 2,000 years, since the Roman invasions of 55 BC. The natives, illiterate tribal peoples, mixed customs with high Roman civilization. These Romanized people then felt the anger of invading German tribes in the 5th century. Then came the Vikings in the 8th and 9th centuries and then the French conquest of 1066. Adding to this complex and mixed culture, there were other native British tribes like the Picts, the Scots and the Welsh who sometimes mixed with the English and sometimes fought with them. Britain was nearly always changing - killing kings, fighting rebels. All of these groups made Britain diverse, powerful and often unstable – basically the opposite of a good, Confucian society. This is especially true when you think of the British tendency to put the needs of individuals above the needs of the nation – a trait they would pass down to the Americans. Robin Hood, King Arthur and a hundred other British popular heroes all fought against society to protect individual people.

And unlike America, Britain has maintained many of these small tribal identities for hundreds of years. Wales, for example, was not a part of the English Empire until nearly the time of Shakespeare. Even during the early 18th century, when England was a great imperialist power, Scotland and Ireland were still independent. The modern United Kingdom, which has existed since only 1922, is actually four countries – Wales, Northern Ireland, Scotland and England - with one government.

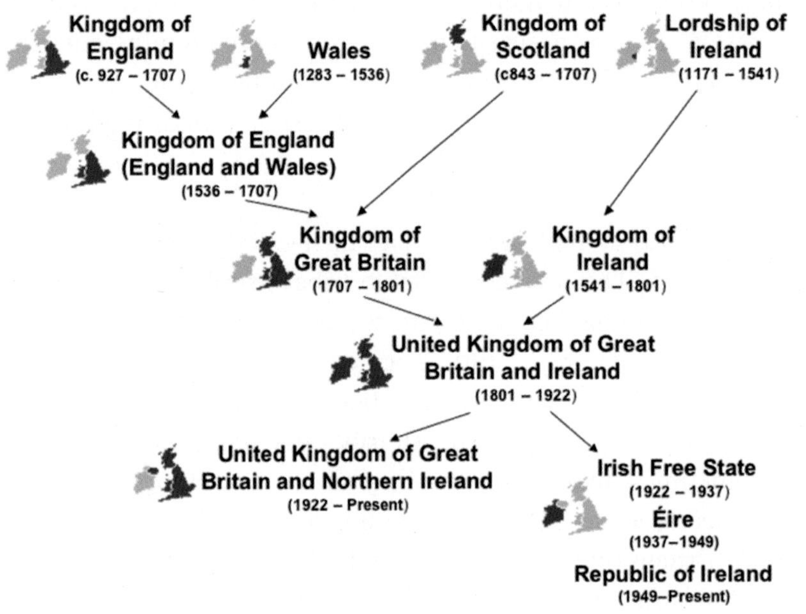

Timeline showing the formation of the modern United Kingdom

But even with all the instability, with all the change, Great Britain has possibly impacted the world more than any other country in the past 300 years. British law forms the basis for American law, Indian law, Australian law and even Korean law. The Japanese government is patterned after Britain, as is the Canadian system and dozens of others. Britain introduced industry to the world – every factory, industrial robot and computer you see today traces its origin to 18th century Great Britain. British music brought us the Beatles, Rolling Stones and Led Zeppelin. British business, beginning with the East India Company, basically invented globalization. British philosophy brought us both John Locke and John Stuart Mill, the people who invented almost everything you are likely to believe about human rights. The British King James brought us the most important version of the Bible. British poetry brought us William Shakespeare, Geoffrey Chaucer and John Milton. British novels include the work of Jane Austen, Charles Dickens and George Orwell. British scientists included Isaac Newton and Edward Jenner, the inventor of vaccination.

From Left - Rock band The Beatles, physicist Isaac Newton, play write William Shakespeare, novelist Jane Austen, the King James Bible, philosopher John Locke. All came from Great Britain.

All this influence is partly because the British made good laws, music, philosophy and literature. It is also partly because no country has ever dominated so many foreigners. British imperialists sometimes exploited, sometimes developed India for more than 200 years. British traders started a war in China so they could sell a drug called opium* and brought literacy to huge areas of Africa.* They gave Australia both civilization and genocide.* They created peaceful nations like Canada but also caused many of the wars still happening in the Middle East.* Finally, England made one country that borrowed an especially huge amount of British law, music, philosophy and literature – the United States.

Group Activity: Debate whether Great Britain did more good or bad for the world. Half of the students should argue that Great Britain was good, half that Britain was bad.

The First World War severely damaged British power but it wasn't until the Second World War that the empire finally ended. Today Great Britain is still a rich, developed country. Its military is still strong and its culture, whether with TV dramas like Sherlock or musicians like Adele, still influences the world. However, it is no longer a superpower. It cannot compete with the United States, China or the former Soviet Union. According to Business Insider, the United Kingdom is currently the fifth strongest military in the world, behind the USA, Russia, China and India.*

Between them, the United States and Britain have dominated the western world for most of the last three hundred years. Why did they become so strong? What do they have in common? Where did they come from? How are they different from the great powers of East Asia?

Group Project: Imagine a world dominated by Asia. What would this look like? What would the consequences be? Make a short presentation in groups of three or four.

Starting next chapter, we will explore these questions by looking at two major struggles. The first is a fight between Anglo-Americans who want to include foreigners and those who want to preserve traditions. This conflict started with the Roman Empire and has lasted more than 2,000 years now. This struggle has shaped everything from feminism to imperialism to democracy. The second is the struggle between Anglo Americans who want strong central power and those who would prefer weak kings or presidents. While Korea has had a strong central government since the beginning of the Unified Shilla period, British and American people have fought and died for almost a thousand years trying to either localize or centralize power. This struggle has changed Anglo-American culture deeply as well. The struggle against central power heavily influenced slavery, libertarianism and Magna Carta. The struggle to for central power was a huge influence on imperialism, civil rights and anti-communism.

Resources	
For more information on the Opium War, visit http://terms.naver.com/entry.nhn?docId=908166&cid=42979&categoryId=42979	
For more information on British-led literacy in Africa, visit http://mpra.ub.uni-muenchen.de/7029/1/MPRA_paper_7029.pdf	
For more information about the British colonization of Australia, visit http://www.nationsonline.org/oneworld/History/Australia-history.htm	
For more information about the British division of the Middle East, visit http://www.thetower.org/article/the-map-that-ruined-the-middle-east/	
For more information about global military strength, visit http://www.businessinsider.com/11-most-powerful-militaries-in-the-world-2014-4	

#1

Britain's Greatest Achievements.	Britain's Biggest Mistakes.
1.	1.
2.	2.
3.	3.
4.	4.
5.	5.

#2

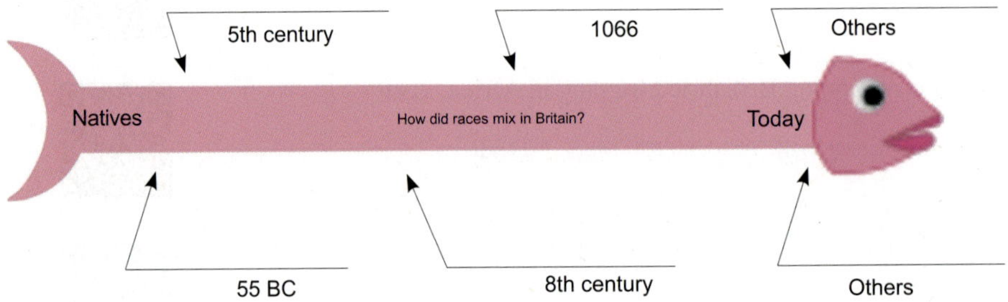

#3

Essay: How did English culture impact Korea?

#4

Take a survey in class. Who is your favorite British athlete? Favorite British actor/actress? Favorite British singer/band? Explain your choices and your reasoning.

03

How the Romans Acculturated Britain

Pre-reading vocabulary and phrases

assimilate	to make someone or something become part of a group, country, society etc.
acculturate:	to change so that you become more like people from a different culture
carrots and sticks	a system in which you are rewarded for some actions and threatened with punishment for others
coercion	the use of force to persuade someone to do something that they are unwilling to do
follow suit	to do the same as someone else has just done

Arnold Schwarzenegger is one of the most successful people in the world. He left his native Austria when he was 21 years old and came to the US, even though he spoke almost no English. In the US, Schwarzenegger won the Mr. Olympia contest for the world's best male body builder seven times. His huge muscles and manly face became the ideal for millions of British and American men.

In his early thirties he became one of the biggest movie stars in the world. He was the lead actor in *Conan the Barbarian*, the first three *Terminator* movies and *Predator*. For more than ten years, he was the most desired action movie star in the world. He later became governor of California and is currently a very successful businessman and publisher.

Hines Ward is also a famous American immigrant. Son of a Korean mother and an African American soldier from the US, Ward left Korea when he was about one year old. Due to his mixed race, people in Seoul would often spit at Ward's mother, Young-he Ward. In the US, Ward struggled with his identity before turning to sports. His mother, mixing American culture with her Korean traditions, was able to give Ward much more stability than many non-immigrant Americans. Hines Ward excelled in baseball and football, eventually joining the Pittsburg Steelers professional football team where he set many records and won two championships. Today, Ward is a successful broadcaster and TV star. He also supports other mixed race, "twigi" children.*

From left - actor, politician and businessman Arnold Schwarzenegger, famous novelist, professor and intellectual Chang-rae Lee and athlete Hines Ward. All immigrated to the United States.

Germaine Lindsay was one of the most dangerous murderers in British history. He exploded himself in Russel Square in London, killing 25 people. Friends described Lindsay as a normal, friendly boy who changed after he took a vacation to Afghanistan. A friend described his change this way. "Jermaine went to the extreme. He became an evil bastard to a lot of people he had grown up with."*

Germaine Lindsay, an immigrant.

What do Arnold Schwarzenegger and Germaine Lindsay have in common? They were both immigrants. Schwarzenegger came from Austria as a young man. He integrated into the US very well. He changed the culture for the better and helped his new country. Lindsay came to the UK from Jamaica as a child and integrated poorly. He caused a devastating attack that killed dozens of people and frightened millions.

Some British and American people say that successful immigrants like Arnold Schwarzenegger, or famous Korean immigrant and novelist Chang-rae Lee, are very important to the US and Britain. They think British and American people should welcome foreigners. They say "look at our diverse food. See how we can eat Mexican food for breakfast, Italian food for lunch and Chinese food for dinner." They say "immigrants help us come up with new ideas, new technologies, new arts." They say "immigrants make us strong. They are movie stars, singers and businessmen. No immigrant families means we would have no Google, no Apple, no Budweiser."

Some British and American people think differently. They say that destructive immigrants like Germaine Lindsay or the killer at Virginia Tech University, are so horrible we should never allow them to immigrate. They also say that immigrants take away British and American traditions. "The English language is so beautiful, but these immigrants don't learn how to speak English. They are ruining our language." "These immigrants are dirty, they don't care about our morals, they want to live like Filipinos or Mexicans, they are criminals. We should get rid of them."

Group Activity: Korea has recently opened to the world. How should Japanese, Chinese and Filipino immigrants to Korea behave? How should native Koreans behave to immigrants? Should the Korean government restrict certain races? Discuss with your classmates.

This disagreement between people who like immigrants and people who oppose immigrants has been going on for 2,000 years. Now that we've studied the modern US and UK, it's important to understand the cultural origin – Rome. Indeed, one secret to Rome's power was how they dealt with immigrants.

There are relatively few empires in history. Rome was probably the greatest, or at least the second greatest, of these empires. How did Rome assimilate and acculturate so many countries? How did the Romans convince so many people to accept their rule? What made Rome so strong? Why did it last so long? Did it ever go away?

We think it's helpful to think of Great Britain as the second version of Rome and the USA as the third version of Rome. We think this because they both use many of the same techniques as Rome, they even controlled many of the same territories. As such, students should pay special attention to this chapter. Most of the stories in this book will refer to the Roman origins of English and American culture.

The Roman Empire lasted more than a thousand years (two thousand years if you count the eastern empire) because they were very good at getting people from many ethnicities, speaking many languages, to identify themselves as Roman. In other words, they were good at destroying local, ethnic identities and replacing them with a larger, pan-Roman identity. But how did this work in Great Britain?

According to the ancient Greek historian Dio, Rome began the process by establishing economic ties between the sophisticated Roman merchants and the tribal, British merchants.* This created personal and business relationships between the two cultures. Think about the consequences of these relationships. Cultures with business connections don't want to fight. Imagine how angry the top officials at Samsung would be if South Korea decided to fight a war with China. There would be an outcry. The same things happened in ancient Britain. Merchants and farmers in Britain needed the Roman market to thrive. Rome used this power to introduce its sophisticated administrative systems. This resulted in British business structures integrating with Roman business structures.

Once they had economic power, the Romans were remarkably flexible with the British. The Roman politicians, business leaders and traders did not try to change British religions, British languages or British political systems. As long as the British were loyal to Rome, Rome did not disturb British society.

Rome was also much more advanced than the British tribes. This allowed them to offer the British people both very appetizing carrots and threaten them with very scary sticks. Basically, Rome could say "we will make you richer and stronger and give you Roman citizenship if you cooperate" but also "if you don' t cooperate, we will kill you with our extremely powerful army." Given Rome' s flexible attitudes and powerful military, cooperation was not a difficult choice for most British people. The people who did resist, Roman soldiers killed.

As soon as the British cooperated, the next part of the Roman strategy became important. As you will read in Niccolo Machiavelli's essay later in this chapter, Rome didn't care about racial purity. Like the modern Americans or British people who want immigrants, the Romans were okay with interracial marriages, new languages and different traditions. Because of this, they would encourage Roman soldiers to marry British women. British men would also go to Rome and marry Roman women. This solidified cultural bonds and allowed the Romans to safely control Britain. In other words, the Romans conquered Britain as much with sex as they did with weapons.

Group project: Is the Roman strategy good for modern times? How can Korea use Roman techniques? What other countries are using Roman techniques on Korea? Discuss with your classmates.

The conquest began in the time of Julius Caesar, 55-54 B.C. However, Rome did not completely control Britain until 43 A.D. when Emperor Claudius finished conquering Britain. The Romans offered many economic advantages to British people. Roman military camps often became cities. London, for example, probably started as a Roman military camp.* This is important because cities were unknown in Britain at the time. As such, when British people accepted Roman rule, they gained huge economic benefits. These benefits included better farm equipment, better farm animals, sophisticated markets for their goods and vastly superior infrastructure. These benefits helped most British people, but the common people in particular.

However, because Rome didn't attack the political structures of cooperating British tribes, British rulers were also able to accept Roman control. Further, when British leaders gave their power to Rome, they got access to the entire empire. A native British person, if they were smart and rich enough, could succeed anywhere in the empire. They could become a general in Spain, a merchant in Egypt or a politician in Greece. The leaders, in other words, had access to much more power inside the Roman system than they did while still independent. For example, native Britain Tiberius Claudius Cogidubnus built several impressive baths, palaces and plazas in the city of Fishbourne, Sallustius Lucullus was an ethnic

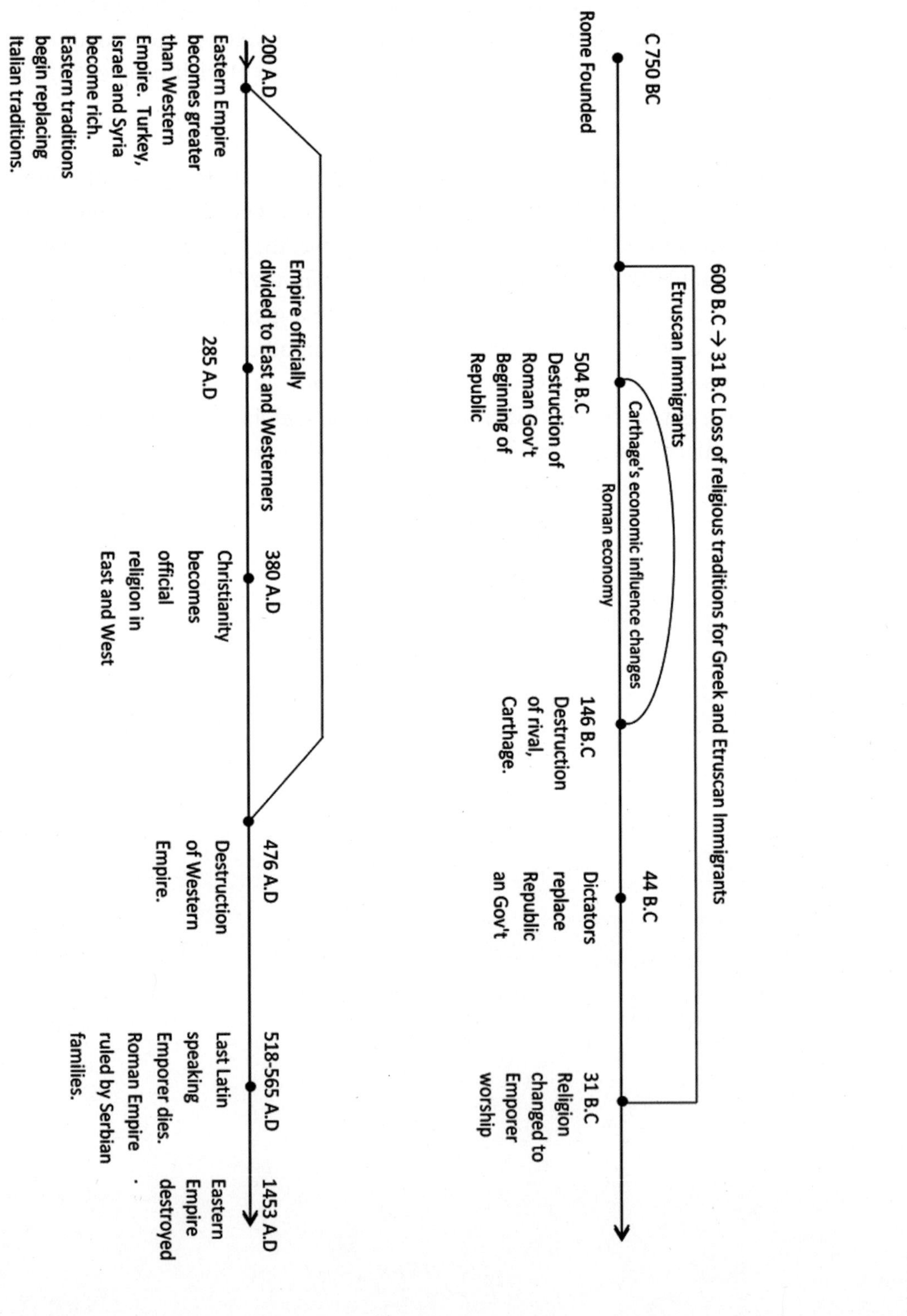
600 B.C → 31 B.C Loss of religious traditions for Greek and Etruscan Immigrants
Etruscan Immigrants
Carthage's economic influence changes
Roman economy
C 750 BC
Rome Founded
504 B.C
Destruction of Roman Gov't Beginning of Republic
146 B.C
Destruction of rival, Carthage.
44 B.C
Dictators replace Republic an Gov't
31 B.C
Religion changed to Emporer worship
Empire officially divided to East and Westerners
200 A.D
Eastern Empire becomes greater than Western Empire. Turkey, Israel and Syria become rich. Eastern traditions begin replacing Italian traditions.
285 A.D
380 A.D
Christianity becomes official religion in East and West
476 A.D
Destruction of Western Empire.
518-565 A.D
Last Latin speaking Emporer dies. Roman Empire ruled by Serbian families.
1453 A.D
Eastern Empire destroyed

Britain who became provincial governor and ethnic Britain Constantine III became emperor of the Western Empire in the early 5th century.

The Roman system for assimilating and acculturating British people was extremely successful. In the time following the conquest, Rome changed Britain from an island full of warring tribes into one of the richest, most prosperous provinces in the Roman Empire. In fact, it may have worked too well. When the Roman Empire began to fall, Britain was still getting stronger and wealthier.

The Roman Empire in 117 A.D. Successful Britons could work and live anywhere they wanted inside the empire – if they were loyal.

On How Rome Became a Great State, Destroying the States That Surrounded It, and How It Took Foreigners Into Its Ranks.

Niccolo Machiavelli

Portrait of Niccolo Machiavelli

니콜로 마키아벨리는 작가이자 철학자이며, 많은 사람들은 그가 정치과학 분야를 발전시켰다고 믿고 있습니다. 그의 성장 시기는 16세기 이탈리아가 약소국이고 분열된 국가였을 때입니다. 그의 가장 유명한 작품들인, "군주론", "왕자와 담론"의 주된 목적은 로마처럼 강해지는 방법을 이탈리아 사람들에게 가르치는 것이었습니다. 이 글은 담론에서 발췌한 것이며, 마키아벨리가 아테네와 스파르타가 영향력 있는 그리스 시대의 제국이었지만 왜 로마제국처럼 오래가지 못했는지 생각하는지를 보여줍니다.

Leaders who want their cities to become great empires must work hard to increase the population of their cities because, without lots of men, the city can never become powerful. The prince can increase his population in two ways: through "love" or through "force." If it is through love, the leader should keep the city open for foreigners to come and welcome everyone. If it is through force, the prince will destroy the nearby cities and force the inhabitants of those cities to live in his own city. Rome used both love and force so diligently that by the time of their sixth king, Rome had 80,000 soldiers. The Romans wanted to act like good farmers. Instead of adding each new city to their empire, they wanted to cut off the first, small branches so that the tree trunk of their country, the city of Rome, could grow stronger.

The examples of Sparta and Athens demonstrate why the prince should use love and force to grown the city. Both Sparta and Athens had powerful armies and excellent laws, and yet they did not reach the greatness of the Roman Empire. They were more orderly, but less powerful. No other reason for Rome's greatness can be put forward than the one I have already suggested: Rome had used both love and force and was able to fight with 80,000 men, while Sparta and Athens never surpassed 20,000 soldiers. This was not because Rome had a better location, only that it had a different way of dealing with foreigners.

King Lycurgus, the founder of Sparta, believed that foreigners would corrupt his laws, and consequently did his best to prevent foreigners mixing with Spartans. Not only did he forbid intermarriage and citizenship for outsiders, but he decided that only leather money could be used in Sparta. He did this in order to discourage merchants from coming to Sparta with goods or crafts. The result was that the city could never grow in population. Since our countries follow the example of nature, it is neither possible nor natural that a delicate trunk (small population) will be able to sustain heavy branches (empire).

Therefore a small republic cannot hope to control cities larger or stronger than it is. If it tries, it will meet the same fate as a tree whose branches are larger than its trunk: it will stand up only with difficulty and break in the smallest breeze.

This was the case of Sparta, which successfully conquered all the other cities in Greece. However, as soon as Thebes (a small Greek city) rebelled, all the other cities followed suit and the trunk remained alone without branches. This could not happen to Rome, as its trunk was so thick that it could support branches of any size. This is what made Rome powerful and great.

Resources	
For more information on Hines Ward's efforts to support mixed race children, visit http://www.nytimes.com/2009/11/09/sports/football/09ward.html?pagewanted=all http://www.koreatimesus.com/hines-ward-the-legend-goes-on/	
For more information on Germaine Lindsey, visit http://www.mirror.co.uk/news/uk-news/exclusive-scent-from-hell-550498	
For more information on London's origins, visit https://books.google.co.kr/books?id=LhEcBQAAQBAJ&lpg=PP10&ots=UuHN3W5swN&pg=PP22&redir_esc=y#v=onepage&q&f=false	
For more information on the early Roman business connections with Britian, see chapters 38, 49 and 51 in Cassius Dio'sHistoriaeRomanae	

#1

Compare and contrast the way Rome dealt with foreigners and the way Heungseon Daewangun dealt with foreigners.

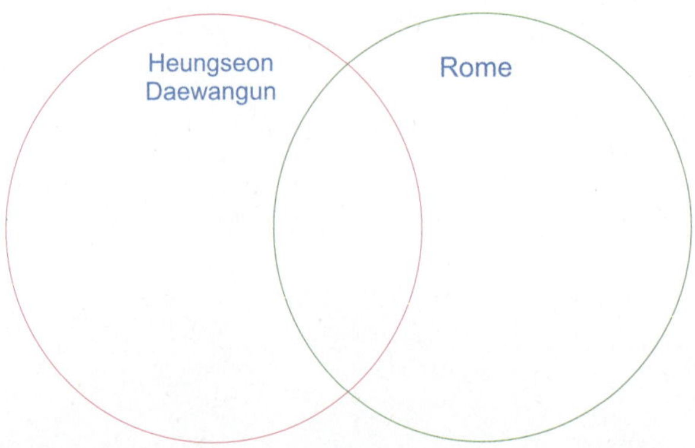

#2

How did Rome conquer Britain?

Cultural ways	Military ways	Other ways
1.	1.	1.
2.	2.	2.
3.	3.	3.

#3

Why is it important Rome didn't try to preserve its racial purity?

#4

What advantages does Heungseon Daewagun's approach have?

#5

What foreign things should Korea block? What should it accept? With a classmate, make a system for deciding how open Korea should be.

#6

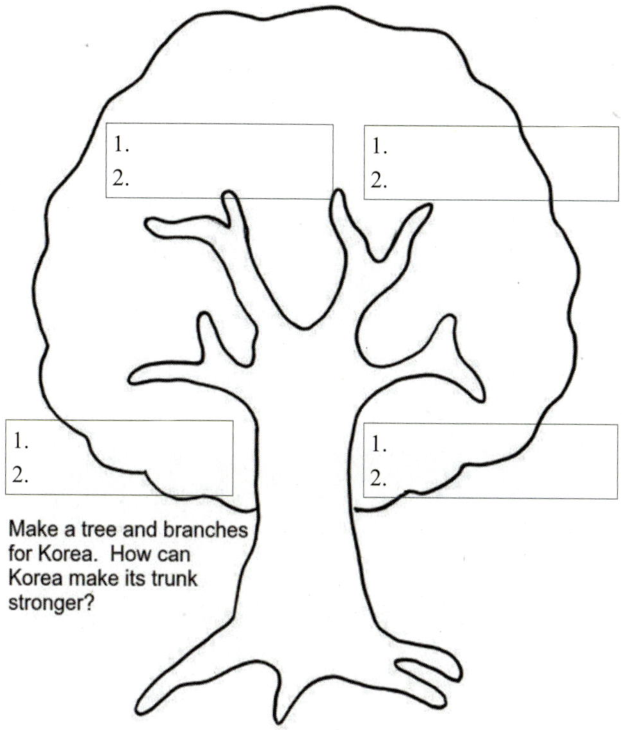

#7

What would the Romans think of Lee Jasmin?

Positive opinions	Negative opinions	Your opinions
1.	1.	1.
2.	2.	2.
3.	3.	3.
4.	4.	4.
5.	5.	5.

04

William the Conqueror

Statue of William the Conqueror

Pre-reading vocabulary and phrases

divine right:	a belief that a king or queen represents, and has been given power by, God
alderman	a member of a local government chosen by the other members
poaching:	to catch and kill animals without permission on someone else's land
pick up (a romantic partner)	to make a romantic connection with a new person
collaborator (politically):	a person who works with an enemy who has taken control of their country

Ben, one of the authors of this book, has a Korean friend who stole a motorcycle. When the police came, this friend tried to escape. While running from the police, he crashed the motorcycle and destroyed it. The police took him to the police station, scolded him and let him go. Ben found this amazing. If this Korean friend had committed those crimes in the US, he would have spent at least a year in jail, probably much longer. Indeed, according to the International Center for Prison Studies, the US imprisons .7% of its population at any given time. That is about 730% more than South Korea.* To explain another way, the New York Times reports that by age 23, about 30% of Americans will have been arrested at least once.*

Consider another example. We'd like you to think about the traffic in Korea. When a traffic light turns red, three or four more cars will go through the intersection, right? If the road signs say only one lane can turn left, how many lanes of traffic will turn left anyway? Two? Three? All of them? When an ambulance comes, how many people move their cars out of the way?

In Korea, traffic laws are less strict. In America, people who ignore a red light can go to jail. In Britain, people who make illegal left turns lose their drivers' licenses. In both countries, if you don't move for an ambulance, the police will fine you very harshly.

Business is similar. In Korea, if a businessman doesn't pay his employees, it's not that big of a deal. Maybe the employees will quit, eventually. Maybe he will pay them later. If a businessman offers a bribe to a government official, it's bad, but the official and the businessman will usually only be fined. Perhaps because of this, Korea ranks only 43rd in global corruption indexes, compared to 17th for the US and 14th for the UK.*

In the US, if a businessman doesn't pay his employees, the government will take the businessman's house away. In England, if a businessman bribes a government official, both of them will go to jail. The government official will never get another government job and the businessman will probably never get another job in business. In really bad cases of bribery, the corrupt people can stay in jail for 20 years or more.

So why are Britain and the US so much harsher with their laws? Why do police punish crimes so strongly? One reason is because British and American people take government laws very seriously. Taking the laws very seriously began, partly, with William the Conqueror.

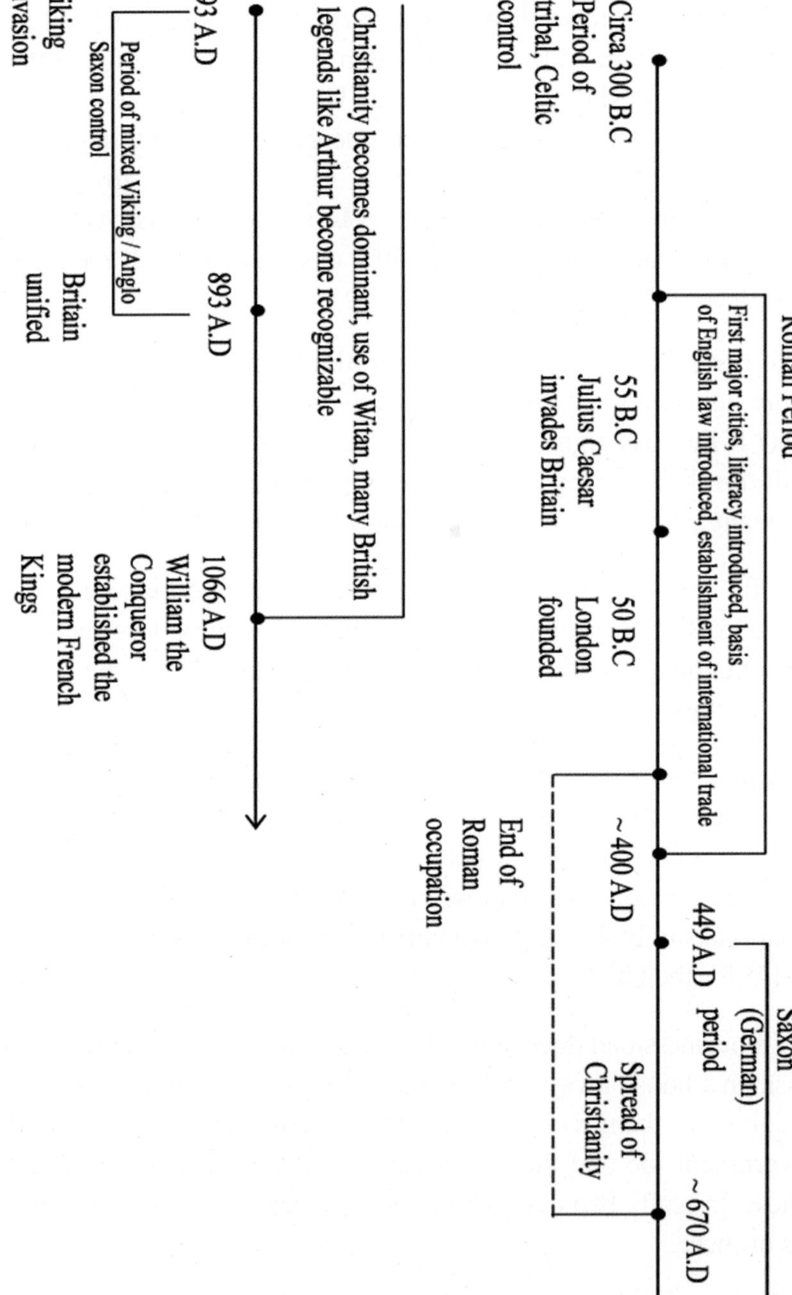
Roman Period
Anglo Saxon (German) period
First major cities, literacy introduced, basis of English law introduced, establishment of international trade
Circa 300 B.C Period of tribal, Celtic control
55 B.C Julius Caesar invades Britain
50 B.C London founded
~ 400 A.D End of Roman occupation
449 A.D
Spread of Christianity
~ 670 A.D
Christianity becomes dominant, use of Witan, many British legends like Arthur become recognizable
793 A.D Viking invasion
Period of mixed Viking / Anglo Saxon control
893 A.D Britain unified
1066 A.D William the Conqueror established the modern French Kings

The last Roman soldiers, due to the collapse of their empire, left Britain in 410 A.D. This left the Celts, Druids (영국의 토착민) and other British tribes alone for the first time in almost 500 years. Because the relationship between Rome and Britain had been so good, most people wanted to continue living Roman-style lives. As such, Britain became a loose kingdom with power divided between local, Roman-style governors and a relatively weak king. They even had a parliament system.

This all came to an end in 1066 when Prince William from Normandy (northern France) killed the last Anglo-Saxon king, Harold, at a battle called Hastings. William did not just conquer, though. He completely changed the fabric of British society. With William came the strict, centralized Norman law and the Norman (French) language. For the first time, Britain's local rulers became weak and the central king became very powerful.

Before William invaded, British kings had no "divine right of kings." While the Anglo-Saxon Witan (a very old parliament) usually chose the son of the previous king, they did not have to. The royal family wasn't special. The Saxon "parliament" was similar to the Roman Senate and was, for the time, fairly sophisticated. When William arrived, he destroyed the Witan and concentrated all power with the king. William's absolute divine right would last for 150 more years before Magna Carta (we'll learn about this in chapter 5) returned some power to the people.

Unlike the more sophisticated system of representatives and aldermen in the Witan, William's Norman system was much cruder. Instead of using different parts of government for local and national problems, William centralized everything. Instead of listening to local representatives and using traditional law, William used power and force to get his way.

As an example of ignoring local leaders and using force, William and the Normans introduced the incredibly unpopular "Forest Law." This law took all of the public property in Britain and made it the King's private land. This badly hurt the normal Anglo-Saxon people who needed public land for very important activities like grazing and hunting. Because Forest Law and William's high taxes were so unpopular, Anglo-Saxon people supported "hero outlaws" like Robin Hood. Because the Normans were so hated, Anglo-Saxon people cheered for criminals who would poach and steal from the Normans. Hero outlaws not only helped

people feed their families, but also acted like revenge against the Normans.
Since the Normans felt unsafe in England, a period of intense castle and wall building began. This is important because castles are almost always the "architecture of fear." Where the Ango-Saxon society had been fairly open, William and the Normans built military buildings all over the country to protect themselves.

Group Project: Do you think the Norman family who lived here felt safe? Why or why not? Work with classmates and guess about the Norman family's circumstances.

Group Project: How about the Roman family that lived in this British villa? Explain why you think they felt safe or unsafe.

The Norman-French language also had a huge effect on the Anglo-Saxon language. Norman French derived words make up as much as 70% of all modern English words. Those words were adapted to Anglo-Saxon pronunciation rules and used with Anglo-Saxon grammar. As the societies mixed, they effectively created a new language so they could communicate. It has been famously said that "the English language is the result of Norman soldiers trying to pick up Saxon waitresses."

It's also the reason why English has two words for everything. Why do English speakers call the living animal a "pig" but a dead one "pork?" Or why is "cow" when it's alive but "beef" when it's inside a hamburger? It's because the Saxon farmers who were raising the animals called them pigs and cows, but the Norman aristocrats who were eating inside their castles called them porks and beefs. A similar phenomenon occurs in curse words. Most "crude" curses are from Anglo-Saxon while most "fine words" are from Norman French.

Finally, while William did cause a great deal of destruction, he was also a builder. By getting rid of the local leaders, William was able to make bigger and more coordinated plans. For example, he was able to plan roads and infrastructure, build a more intelligent military system and create the "Doomsday Book," which made a list of all the property and owners in Britain. Because of this, Britain became more powerful and, in many ways, more efficient. A respect for the government's laws, and harsh punishments, partially started with him.

Please watch this documentary on William the Conqueror:

http://www.youtube.com/watch?v=gItfGVaRnZo	http://www.youtube.com/watch?v=VV1ujajcPa0	http://www.youtube.com/watch?v=UrXAVYEy-fs

Resources

For more information on prison populations worldwide, visit. http://www.prisonstudies.org/highest-to-lowest/prison_population_rate?field_region_taxonomy_tid=All	
For more information about the numbers of Americans who've gone to jail, visit. http://www.nytimes.com/2011/12/19/us/nearly-a-third-of-americans-are-arrested-by-23-study-says.html?_r=0	
For more information about corruption, visit http://www.transparency.org/country#GBR_DataResearch	

#1

What can you infer about these societies? All pictures are of kings'/presidents' homes.

Royal Palace of Rabat (Morocco)

Iranian leader Imam Khomeini's house

Lee Kuan Yew's house (Signapore)

British PM's house

#2

What laws are too relaxed in Korea? Ask at least 3 classmates for ideas. Present your findings.

#3

William's message was clear, "collaborate or die." How is this similar to Rome? How is it different?

#4

William wanted absolute power for the king. What are good and bad consequences for this?

good	bad
1.	1.
2.	2.
3.	3.
4.	4.
5.	5.

05

Magna Carta

An original copy of Magna Carta, the most important constitution in history.

Pre-reading vocabulary and phrases

reign	a period of time when a king or queen rules a country
livelihood	the money people need to pay for food, a place to live, clothing, etc
dirty work:	and unpleasant or dishonest job
habeas corpus:	legal order that states that a person in prison must appear before and be judged by a court of law before he or she can be forced by law to stay in prison
due process:	a citizen's fair treatment within the rules of a government's legal system

Imagine that the police come to your house and say you are a thief. They want to punish you, so they break your TV. They put you in prison with no trial. When they finally release you, you find that the military is camping in your place of employment and using your computer. Imagine if there were no lawyers, no courts, no rights. This sounds pretty terrible, doesn't it? Unfortunately, this was the normal way of doing things in many "divine right" societies and it didn't change until Magna Carta.

In the US and Britain, people are very enthusiastic about rights. They believe in a right to privacy, a right to dignity. They believe in rights to property and the right to choose your religion. Americans and British people very strongly protect the right to criticize the government or the president whenever you want.

Americans and British people believe very strongly in the right to free speech. They can say that Barack Obama is a servant of the devil, former British Prime Minister Tony Blair is a murderer and that George Bush is like Hitler. The government cannot punish them for doing this.

Modern South Korea believes in rights, too, though maybe not as much. The American and British versions of free speech are much stronger than South Korean free speech.* According to Reporters without borders, South Korea is 57th in free speech, while the US is 46th and the UK is 33rd.* The president of the

USA, for example, could never force Saturday Night Live to say nice things about him. The Prime Minister of Great Britain could never arrest someone for "insults."

Group Project: Imagine that South Korea had free speech rights like the US and England. Discuss with your classmates how this would make Korea better and how it would make Korea worse.

However, these ideas are relatively new in Korea and most Koreans think they come from the government. "The South Korean government gives me the right to choose my religion." In the West, many people believe that these rights come from nature or from God. "God gives me the right to speak in any way I want and the government can NEVER control what I want to say."

Where did these rights come from? Partially they came from that 1,000 year old fight between people who want local control and the people who want central control. Rights, advocates of local control thought, could limit the power of the king or president and help local leaders.

Even more than the advocates for local control, though, the idea of using laws to control the government came from a very important constitution that Bishop Stephen Langton and the English invented in 1215. Almost every constitution on earth, including the Korean and American constitutions, is based on Stephen Langton's constitution, Magna Carta.

From the time of William the Conqueror until 1215, the King of England ruled by divine right. With divine right, a king can change or break the laws whenever he wants because, everyone believes, the king's power comes from God. This changed because the last British king with divine right, John (1166-1216), was an incredibly poor leader.

Group Project: Imagine you and your classmates are given divine right in Korea. What would you do?

King John became the king in 1199 and ruled until his death in 1216. At this time, the English kings had traditionally also controlled Normandy in France. However, early in King John's reign, King Philip II, a French King from Paris, conquered Normandy and took those lands from John. Philip II succeeded for a number of reasons. First, John was cruel to the Normans in France and the nobles in England. As such, those people did not want to support King John. Secondly, he did not have enough money or soldiers. John's poor leadership would make both of those problems worse as his reign continued.

First, he forced the English nobles to collect very high taxes. Because nobles were responsible for taking taxes from the regular citizens, this made the citizens very angry at the nobles. The nobles, in turn, became angry at King John for requiring so much "dirty work." King John wanted the high taxes so that he could attack France and take back his land in Normandy.

His invasion, however, failed. King John responded to his failure by raising taxes even more and making laws so that people could only use police or courts if they had enough money to pay the king. He would attempt several more invasions of France, failing each time.

*Bishop Stephen Langton, the man most responsible for Magna Carta.**

King John also started a fight with the Pope when he tried to choose officials for the Catholic Church. When John interfered with the election of Bishop Stephen Langton, a very unpopular conflict began. The Pope closed all the churches in England for three years. Today, closing all the churches would be very annoying but, in the 13th century, people believed that if they couldn't go to church, they would go to hell. John's fight with the Pope therefore caused a huge panic among the people.

Because John continually ignored the wishes and advice of the nobles, the church members and the general population, Stephen Langton and some of the nobles started a revolt in 1215. While these rebels were able to capture London, they were not strong enough to completely defeat John. In the end, they offered to stop fighting if King John signed Magna Carta. Pay special attention to the way Magna Carta law differs from divine right.

*Magna Carta**

To John, the rightful King of England, Lord of Ireland and ruler of Northern France,

We, your loyal bishops, abbots, earls, justices, foresters, sheriffs and servants wish to greet you. We wish to speak to you so we can make our souls healthier, make our church healthier and better organize our kingdom. We write this letter to you on the advice of Stephen Langton, Archbishop of Canterbury, Henry, archbishop of Dublin and … (Magna Carta lists 26 more church leaders and nobles).

Introduction: These people are the most important players in the revolt. King John and Stephen Langton, Bishop of Cantebury, are the leaders of the two sides. The others are mostly church officials and nobles. Notice how the nobles call themselves "loyal" even though they were in a revolt against King John. This is because they want to return to peace and keep John as their king. This is because not all of the nobles had rebelled. If they had, there probably would not have been a Magna Carta and the nobles would have simply killed King John.

First, we declare that the English Church must be free from the king's influence forever. We declare this because before our current dispute, there was never an attempt by kings to interfere with the church's elections and by the declaration of Pope Innocent III. We will insist on this freedom for ourselves and for our heirs in the future.

This says that the Catholic Church in England is free from the King's power. According to Magna Carta, the church can ignore the king's preference and choose whomever they like as bishop. You can tell how important Bishop Stephen Langton was. His biggest concern is the first part of Magna Carta.

We also declare that all the free men and all the heirs of free men will enjoy the liberties written out below:

The second paragraph extended freedoms originally given only to the nobles to include "all free men" forever. At the time, "free men" were about 10% of the

* 1215년 영국의 귀족들이 존 국왕에게 강요하여 서명하게 한, 영국 국민의 법적 및 정치적 권리 확인서, 흔히 영국 현대법의 기초로 여겨짐. 출처-Oxford Dictionary

청색 글로 쓰여진 문서는 원본이며 굵게 쓰여진 문서는 단순화된 버전입니다. 원본의 대헌장(Magna Carta)*이 너무 어려우시다면 단순화된 버전도 동일 내용을 포함하고 있으므로, 단순화된 버전인 검정색 볼드체만 읽어 보셔도 됩니다.

population. However, over time, the term "free man" changed to include almost every English citizen.

Ordinary lawsuits shall not need to follow the king's court. Instead, legal courts and ordinary lawsuits must be in a permanent location.Local matters like inheritance cases, death certificates and petty complaints shall happen in local courts, not the king's court. We will send two representatives from the central court to the local courts twice a year to ensure the local courts are behaving responsibly.

This is the idea of making a permanent court. Before Magna Carta, the court followed the king wherever he went. There was no place to store legal records. This made it very difficult to schedule lawsuits. It also specifies that the central court will control the local courts to ensure consistency.

For small offences, free men should only receive small fines. For serious offences, free men should get heavier offences, but never so heavy that he loses his livelihood. Courts cannot take a merchant's merchandise, a farmer's farming tools or a shepherd's animals. There can be no fines without the permission of official's who are under oath.

These ensure that punishment is proportional to the crime. For minor crimes, the court cannot give a punishment so strong it will destroy the criminal's livelihood. It also says that you cannot be punished for a crime if there aren't witnesses who swear to tell the truth.

Nobles should be fined only by other nobles, and only in ways that match their offense.

This is an early conception of a jury. Just like you have a right to a "jury of your peers," Magna Carta lets nobles and church people be judged by people like them. Before, only kings or high nobles could judge lower people.

Sheriffs, policemen and royal officials should never decide lawsuits that rightly belong to the king's court.

This says that certain types of legal problems will be handled by local courts, but that everything will be supervised by the main court. The main court would send auditors four times a year to make sure the local courts were being fair.

Police investigations and court trials will always be free. The police and courts shall never refuse to investigate or judge serious criminal cases … Justice shall not be sold. We shall not deprive justice to those who cannot pay for it. We will not delay justice or ignore the rights of free men.

This says that access to justice – police and courts – is always free. Before, because of John's laws, if you didn't have enough money to pay the king, you could not use the courts or police services.

In the future, there will be no trials unless the accuser can produce witnesses and evidence. Simply accusing another person is not sufficient to bring a case to trial.

This says that no serious punishment can be given to a criminal without an official investigation. The investigation must not cost anything for the people involved. This is the predecessor to *habeas corpus*.

No free man can be imprisoned, fined or punished or harmed in any way except after he has been given a chance to defend himself. He may only be punished by his equals or by the law of the land.

This outlines a key part of what we now call due process. Many of the nobles thought this was one of the most important parts of Magna Carta, since it got rid of King John's arbitrary use of the law.

We will only appoint men who know the law and promise to protect the law to be judges, policemen, sheriffs or public officials.

This sets standards for police and legal officials. They must "know the law" and "keep it well" or they cannot hold office. Before, under King John's law, the most important qualification for being a policeman or legal official was not knowledge or honesty, it was simply being friends with King John.

All the rights and privileges we give ourselves we also give to our subordinates. Let the other church officials, nobles and laymen similarly give these rights and privileges to their subordinates as well.

This means that all the freedoms and laws that restrict the king also restrict the nobles. That means, just like the king cannot take a noble's land without legal permission, a noble cannot take his servant's house without permission. This became one of the most historically important parts of Magna Carta because future lawmakers used it to grant many freedoms to normal people.

Resources	
For more information about free speech rankings, visit https://rsf.org/index2014/en-index2014.php	
For more information about Stephen Langton, visit http://magnacarta800th.com/schools/biographies/magna-carta-bishops/stephen-langton/	

#1

Survey Questions

a) What is more important, individual freedom or group cohesion?

b) How dangerous are too many freedoms? (1-10)______________

#2

Research Jo Gwang-jo. Compare his ideas with Stephen Langton.

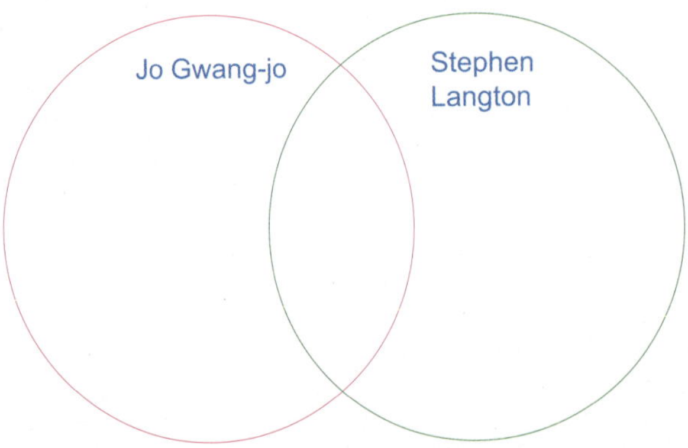

Jo Gwang-jo

#3

With classmates, act out the following scenario: You are a lawyer and your friend is accused of theft. There is some evidence, but the police keep it a secret. How can you defend your friend without the Magna Carta's protections?

#4

Essay: Rome's innovation was assimilating foreigners. William's innovation was centralized power. What is Magna Carta's innovation?

#5

France, Spain and Russia kept divine right for hundreds of years longer. Research one of those countries and explain how divine right helped or hurt them. Present your findings.

#6

Explain the common points and differences between the Magna Carta and Hammurabi's Code.

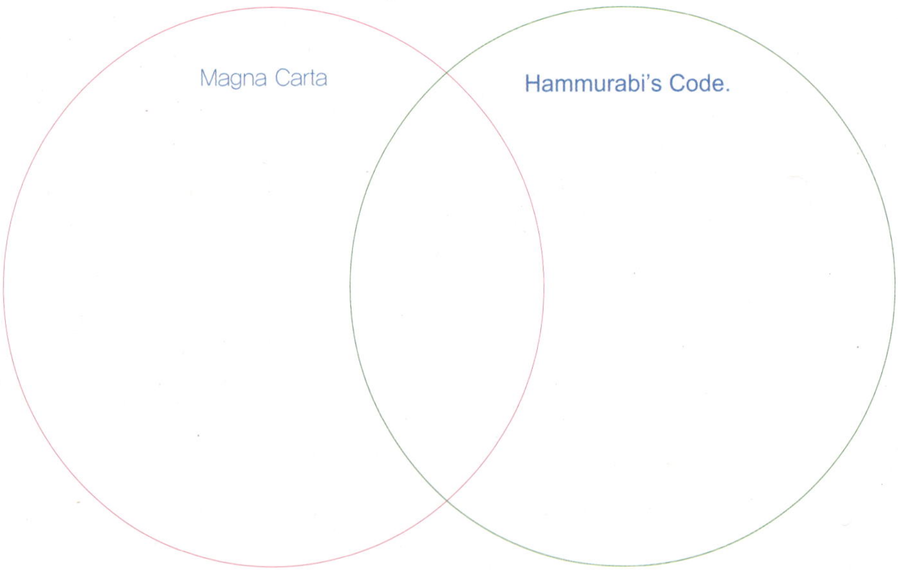

06

Mary, Elizabeth and Femininity

Queen Elizabeth I

Edward IV and his father, Henry VIII, crushing the Pope

Catholic Queen Mary

Pre-reading vocabulary and phrases

protestant	a member of one of the Christian Churches that separated from the Roman Catholic Church during the 16th century
heir	someone who will get another person's money and things when that person dies
Anglican	belonging or relating to the Church of England
don't feel like	to not want to do something
meme	an idea, image, video, etc that is spread very quickly on the internet

How do you think men and women should behave? In traditional Confucian culture, the answer is pretty simple – a woman should support the older men in her family, try to be beautiful, and teach morality to the children. A man should lead the family, work outside of the house and take responsibility for dangerous tasks. Even today, this is a very common Korean expectation.

Traditionally, British and American people had similar expectations. However, this expectation has changed dramatically in the West. The new attitudes about men and women are much more equal, much freer, much scarier for many people.

Traditional British woman shows her weakness.

One example of these new ideas comes from popular writer Linda Hirshman. She says husbands are a danger to women's careers. She says, accurately, that most men expect their wives to sacrifice their careers to help the man. Women, then, should marry men from lower social classes. If an ambitious woman marries a weak, poor man, she can more easily force him to take care of children and do housework.* Similar ideas have become very popular among rich white women in the United States and Great Britain, along with humorous memes like "I drink male tears" and "misandry is magic."*

Group project: What do you think of Hirshman's idea? Male students should argue for Hirshman and female students should argue against her.

Religion also is very often a cause of conflict. In England in 2013, Muslim men in London came onto the streets and yelled at passing Christians, atheists and others. "Obey Islamic law! You must obey our Islamic law! This is a Muslim street!" These people want to change all the government in England so that it is controlled by Islamic, religious laws.*

English Christians, atheists and others were very angry. Many of them want to force the Muslims to leave Britain. Others think British people should understand Muslims and leave them alone. Others want to force Muslims to change their culture.

Group Project: What would you do if those Muslims came to your city?

Queen Elizabeth I faced both the problem of religion and the problem of sexism. Her solutions would influence British and American thinking for hundreds of years. Her decisions would influence both feminism and religious freedom. Let's find out why. We'll start with Elizabeth's father, Henry VIII.

Until the Tudor Dynasty in the 16th century, no woman had ever ruled England. By the end of the 16th century, three had become ruler and it all starts with the famous marriage problems of King Henry VIII.

King Henry VIII really, really wanted a son. If he had no sons, the country would have to be ruled by a woman. Women were weak, stupid and dependent, Henry thought. They could not think logically or be trusted with important decisions. As such, he was in a panic because his first wife kept having daughters.

He wanted to divorce her and marry a young woman named Anne Boleyn so they could have a son. This caused a major problem because, in order to divorce his first wife, Henry needed to seek permission from the Pope. The Pope had not felt like cooperating. After a period of negotiation and argument, Henry gave up trying to convince the Pope.

Henry finally solved this problem by making a new religion, called the Anglican Church, of which Henry was master. This made England officially a protestant country, even though most of the citizens were Catholic. Henry eventually used his power in the Anglican Church to marry, execute and divorce several more women, one of whom had a son named Edward. Because he was a boy, Henry was finally satisfied with his succession.

Group Project: Discuss with classmates why succession isn't important in modern societies. Should it be more important?

After Henry died, 14 year-old Edward became king and he launched the Protestant Reformation, which used force to convert the English people from Catholicism to Anglicanism. His soldiers ran through the country, destroying Catholic churches and killing some Catholics. However, Edward became very sick and died only one year later. This caused a major political crisis in the country. Edward didn't have any children and there were no other male heirs to the throne. This meant that, when he was dying, he would have to choose either one of Henry's daughters, Elizabeth or Mary, or a female cousin named Jane Grey. Mary was the closest relation, but she was Catholic and Edward wanted to destroy Catholicism in England. Jane Grey was only 15 years-old and didn't want to be queen, but at least she was a protestant. He did not seriously consider Elizabeth, eventually choosing Jane Grey.

However, Jane Grey was only queen for nine days before Mary gathered the Catholic forces and took power. Mary tried to destroy Protestantism in England and restore Catholicism. She did this by marrying the King of Spain (a powerful Catholic) and by executing Protestants. This earned her the nickname "Bloody Mary." This means that, in only a few years, British people faced a purge against Catholics and then a purge against Protestants. Religious violence was threatening to destroy the country.

Mary and the King of Spain were unable to have a baby and, when Mary became sick, Elizabeth was the only person eligible to become ruler of England. Elizabeth finally brought stability to the religion problem by saying, in effect, that the English government didn't care what religion the people believed in. This was a key innovation at the time and highly unusual. In Spain, for example, there was the Inquisition to get rid of all non-Catholics. In the Americas, missionaries often used force to make the Indians change their religions, so Elizabeth was exceptionally liberal for the time.

Elizabeth was also unusual in that she did almost everything a "proper" woman of the time wasn't supposed to do. She liked to debate. She would intimidate men who challenged her. She once rode a horse onto a battlefield in a suit of armor. She ruthlessly killed political enemies like the Queen of Scots. Elizabeth's reign, for the first time in English history, challenged the role of women as passive, weak and dependent.

That is not to say Elizabeth always acted like a man, however. One of the nicknames Elizabeth earned was the "Virgin Queen" because she never married and never had children. She very well may have died a virgin, though that's impossible to know for sure.

By all accounts, Elizabeth was sexually interested in men but she also understood that getting married or having a baby would undermine her ability to rule England. According to the rules of society at the time, any husband would have taken her power and become the true ruler of England. If she'd had a baby while unmarried, it would have been a severe scandal dangerous to the country.

As such, Elizabeth used the possibility of marriage to control diplomacy. She was always giving the French hints that if they were just a little bit more generous with trade agreements or alliances, Elizabeth might be interested in one of the French princes. She did the same thing to the Spanish and many other countries – always using the possibility of marriage to gain greater advantages for her country.

By the time of Elizabeth's death, England had enjoyed almost forty years of economic growth, relative peace and cultural development. Her reign had provided the prosperity necessary for artists like William Shakespeare and John Donne, scientists and philosophers like Francis Bacon and explorers like Walter Raleigh and Francis Drake. This was largely because Elizabeth, a woman who Henry thought "silly and irresponsible," had managed to use her femininity as a weapon to control her European rivals.

Roles Powerful Women Play

A trope is a definitional shortcut to explaining something. If we begin a story with the phrase "it was a dark and stormy night," you will know this is a horror story. Similarly, if you watch the TV and see an extremely happy man displaying a vacuum cleaner, you will immediately know the TV is showing an advertisement. Tropes also apply to people. We have included three common tropes that get attached to powerful women along with the explanations for what they mean.

Typical femmes fatale. These women are always attractive but definitely dangerous.

The Femme Fatale– This is a woman who uses her powers of sexual attraction to capture and destroy men. She is usually not totally evil, but her motives are definitely suspicious and she is always manipulative. In fiction, the femme fatale usually tests or tempts the male hero. A good example of this is Catwoman– she's not exactly evil, but Catwoman is definitely dangerous to Batman.

However, in real life, powerful women are sometimes treated like real femmes fatale. Indeed, during King Henry's life, the British people were extremely afraid of having a queen. The reason they were afraid is that they thought a woman, given power, would immediately become evil, manipulative and sexually immoral. They would become "she-wolves," to use the trope-name of the day.

Real, powerful women who became femme fatales in the public imagination include Egyptian Queen Cleopatra, Chinese Emperor Wu Zetien (측천무후) and Queen Elizabeth's rival, the infamous Mary Queen of Scots. A more modern example would be the spy Anna Chapman.

Examples of the Nurse Ratched– unattractive, cruel and severe.

The Nurse Ratched–This trope is named after one of the villains in the popular book "One Flew Over the Cuckoo's Nest." In one sense, the Nurse Ratched is the opposite of the femme fatale. While the femme fatale is extremely feminine, dangerously feminine, the Nurse Ratched makes a mockery of femininity. Where the femme fatale is sexy, the Nurse Ratched is repulsive. Where the femme fatale uses temptation to manipulate men, the Nurse Ratched uses cruelty and force.

In another sense, though, the Nurse Ratched's characteristics are grotesque distortions of the femme fatale's qualities. Where the femme fatale destroys men because she wants to get more power, money or fame, the Nurse Ratched destroys men because she enjoys inflicting pain.

In real life, Queen "Bloody" Mary, the queen of England before Elizabeth I, was viewed as a Nurse Ratched by the English people due to her bloody purge of protestants. Other examples of powerful women seen as Nurse Ratcheds are former Soviet official Rozalia Zemlachka and Queen Ranavalona I of Madagascar.

Representations of the Mother to Her People – this trope is defined by toughness, seriousness and a matronly attitude.

The Mother to Her People –This trope is much more positive than the Nurse Ratched or femme fatale tropes. For a powerful woman to become mother to her people, she must be viewed as feminine, but in a very specific way. Where the femme fatale is sexy and the Nurse Ratched is deeply unsexy, the mother to her people is matronly.

Like a good parent, the mother to her people guides the citizens with a firm hand. She loves her people, but believes it is more important to be strong and fair than it is to be affectionate. Like a good mother, she is fiercely protective of her children, she is impossible to manipulate and deeply self-possessed. While it would be unwise to attack a mother to her people personally, it would be extremely unwise to attack the mother to her people's citizens. The mother to her people is never needlessly cruel, but she won't hesitate to destroy those who threaten her "children."

In real life, Queen Elizabeth I was seen this way. Other examples include German Chancellor Angela Merkel, Queen Zenobia of Palmyra, Queen Seondeok of Shilla and French warlord Joan of Arc.

These tropes are different from the tropes male leaders tend to fall under. It is difficult to imagine, for example, a female leader who is weak and stupid remaining leader for very long. A bored, spoiled woman who doesn't take her position seriously, also, is hard to picture. Why do you think that is?

Resources	
For more information on Linda Hirshman, see her book "Get to Work" or visit http://www.slate.com/blogs/xx_factor/2014/11/18/harvard_business_school_study_it_s_not_kids_but_husbands_that_hold_women.html	
For more information on second wave feminism, visit http://www.slate.com/blogs/xx_factor/2014/08/08/ironic_misandry_why_feminists_joke_about_drinking_male_tears_and_banning.html	
For more information about Muslim protestors in Britain, visit http://www.mirror.co.uk/news/uk-news/muslim-brick-lane-protest-muslim-2926404	

#1

For Male Students: If you were a woman in 17th century England, how would Elizabeth have made you feel?

For Female Students: If you were a man in 17th century England, how would Elizabeth have made you feel?

#2

Religious conflict in England came from a number of sources. Which 4 sources do you think are most important?

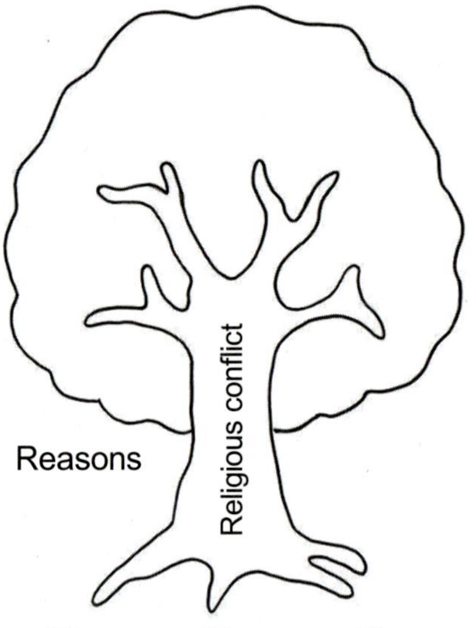

#1______2#_______#3_______4#_________

#3

Elizabeth didn't get married because she wanted power. Many modern people also sacrifice family for their careers. Is this a good decision?

#4

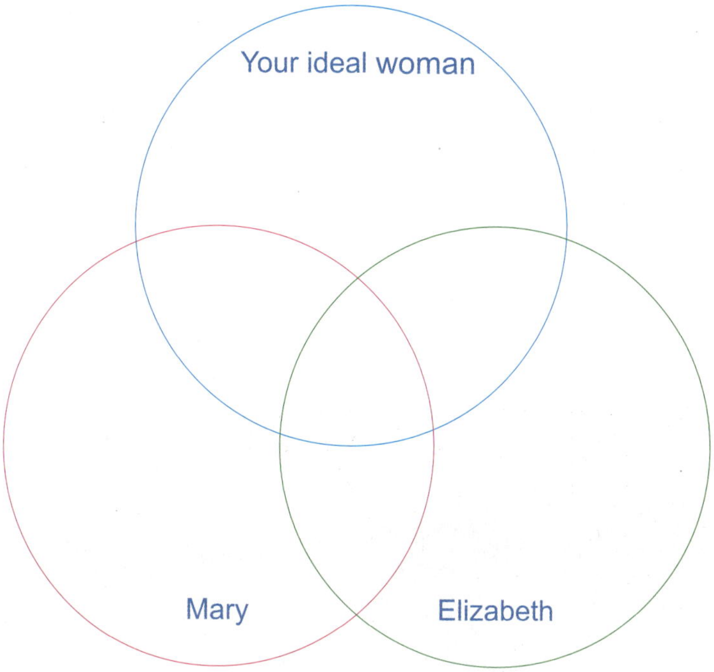

#5

Does Elizabeth remind you of Queen Seondeok? Why or why not? Make sure to research Queen Seondeok.

07

William Penn, Andrew Jackson and the Native Americans

Painting of four Iroquios kings who travelled to London in 1710.

Pre-reading vocabulary and phrases

Quaker	a member of a Christian group, the Society of Friends, that does not have formal ceremonies or a formal system of beliefs and is strongly opposed to violence and war
savage	a violent and uncivilized person
shrewd	able to judge a situation well and get an advantage from it
imperialism	a system in which a country rules other countries, sometimes having used force to get power over them
mutilate	to damage someone's body violently and severely, often by cutting off a part of it
atrocity	an extremely cruel, violent or shocking act
harbor fugitives	to protect and/or hide a person who is being pursued by the police
pacifism	the belief that war is wrong, and, therefore, that to fight in a war is wrong
ethnic cleansing	the organized, often violent attempt by a particular cultural or racial group to completely remove from a country or area all members of a different group

According to the American Bureau of Indian Affairs, there are 566 Native American nations inside the US. Long ago, these people spoke hundreds of different languages. Some of them lived in teepees and hunted buffalo. Some lived in "long houses" in the Pacific forests. Some built clay homes on the sides of cliffs. These days, however, if you visit an Indian village, everyone will speak English, everyone will live in an apartment or house. All the Native Americans will use US dollars to buy things, they will all shop in grocery stores. They will work in factories, warehouses and casinos. What happened to the old variety?

City-on-a-cliff in the southwestern US. Pueblo Indians built these structures.

In 1492, when Christopher Columbus discovered North America, there were about 5,000,000 Native Americans in the modern USA. Disease and war very nearly drove them extinct. In 1910, fewer than 300,000 survived. Their numbers have gone back up and now there are about 3,000,000 Native Americans in the USA. However, even this is less than 1% of the population of the United States.

Americans also deliberately destroyed Indian cultures. Until the 1960s and 1970s, many American states forced Native American children to leave their tribes and enter special schools that taught them how bad Indian culture was. Americans repeatedly took Indian land to give to farmers. American presidents often forced a tribe that lived in the forest to move to the desert, or a desert tribe to move to a swamp. This killed many Indians and destroyed many traditions.

From left to right - Native American comedian and novelist Sherman Alexie. Olympic gold medalist and professional baseball/basketball/football player Jim Thorpe, a member of the Sac and Fox tribe. The United States' first prima ballerina, Maria Tallchief, from the Osage tribe.

However, Americans were not always bad to the Native Americans. Since the 1970s Americans have given land and money to Native American tribes. Native American stories have become popular in mainstream culture and Native American art forms, like dream-catchers, are in demand. Today, many white Americans go to Native American villages to experience traditional religious ceremonies.* As seen in the pictures above, several Native Americans have become famous and influential in mainstream US culture.

Today the relationship between Native Americans and other Americans is complicated. Many Native Americans are still angry at white people for destroying their cultures, killing their ancestors and taking their traditional lands. Many others are angry at modern, non-native Americans for appropriating Native American culture.*

Group Project: How do you feel about the Japanese attacking Korean culture? How do you feel about the South Korean soldiers who attacked Vietnamese culture? If your feelings are different, explain why.

Traditional Native American sweat lodge. This is a kind of sauna some Native Americans use for religious ceremonies. Many Native Americans are angry that people from other cultures perform the religious ceremony without understanding it.

Dream catchers. A Native American type of artwork intended to catch bad dreams.

Koreans have had a similar experience. When the Japanese army ended the Joseon Dynasty, they had vastly more power than the Koreans. Just like the white settlers, the Japanese could do whatever they wanted with the native population. While the Japanese ultimately decided to try and replace Korean culture with Japanese culture, white settlers did many different things all at once. Let's explore William Penn's strategy first.

William Penn's Last, Delightful Asylum

William Penn makes peace with the Delaware Indians.

William Penn, out of all the major white settlers in English America, probably had the best relations with the American Indians. To understand why, it's important to connect William's religious beliefs with the continuing religious crises in England. William Penn, when he was a young man, converted to being a Quaker, a type of pacifist Christian. He also rebelled against English religious authorities, who wanted to control the way people think. Penn became a non-conformist and advocate for religious pluralism. This upset the religious leaders in England, who arrested and imprisoned Penn several times. This suffering made Penn an early advocate for religious freedom and tolerance. In contrast with most Christians of the time, Penn believed that non-Christians deserved religious freedom, too.

These beliefs shaped his behavior in America, where he founded the state of Pennsylvania. While he did want to rule Pennsylvania and spread Quaker beliefs, he was also a pacifist. This meant that instead of fighting the American Indians to take their land, he simply bought the land from them. In order to keep peace, he preferred to treat Indians fairly and to integrate them into his society.

While many of the previous relationships between white men and Indians had been violent, it is important to remember that there were many groups of white men and many Indian tribes. Each group behaved differently at different times. Indeed, there were many cases of certain Indian tribes trading peacefully with certain white settler groups – many white settler groups that saw the Indian tribes as business partners rather than frightening savages.

Penn had to deal most often with the Delaware Tribe, who had never lost a fight against white settlers. While their strength made it a bad idea to fight in general, Penn's experience of religious persecution and his belief in pacifism made him even less inclined to fight. He used "chains of friendship," trusting business relationships, to buy the land from Indians and make a new homeland for Quakers.

Penn was generally a better negotiator than the other white settlers. He accepted the unusual Indian rules of ownership (some pieces of land, under Indian law, had many owners, for example) and gave respect to the Delaware tribe. He was not, however, above using Indian rivalries to his advantage. A shrewd businessman, he would often befriend both sides in an Indian war and offer to buy land from the winner. He also rewarded Indians who traded with him while refusing to deal with Indians who supported his rivals.

Penn made a treaty with the Delaware Indians in 1682. With this, he created a chain of friendship. He used this chain of friendship to buy thousands of square kilometers more land at fair prices.

Sadly, one reason Penn was able to buy the land so easily is because the Indians had been devastated with disease. Unfamiliar bacteria and viruses from Europe and Asia killed hundreds of thousands of Indians, making them weaker and more willing to sell land.

Group Project: Discuss with classmates whether it's a good idea to buy another country's land. If Japan had treated Joseon like Penn treated the Indians, buying Korean land and peacefully replacing Korean culture, would that have been a good thing?

By the end of his career, Penn had outmaneuvered his rivals in New York and Baltimore to create a large, peaceful and prosperous colony. In Pennsylvania, the Quakers were able to escape religious persecution, businessmen were able to build rich cities and the Indians could live in "the last, delightful asylum." The Indians lost their power and their land, but they were not mistreated once Penn gained imperial control. Because of the enduring good relationship, the continued chains of friendship, Pennsylvania Quakers got access to valuable trading routes and also maintained peace with the Indians for almost 100 years.

Penn was an imperialist, but he was also a religious pluralist. Though he planned to make himself "king" of Pennsylvania, he was not unfair. While he had the same goals as most imperialists, he was kinder and gentler than most of his competitors.

If Penn represented the peaceful mixing of a strong outside culture with a weaker native group, the next man we will study represents the opposite.

Andrew Jackson, Eliminating the Indians and Preserving the White Race

Andrew Jackson has an odd legacy. On one hand, his picture is on the twenty-dollar bill, there are hundreds of statues and paintings showing his image. He is celebrated for taking control of the United States away from elites and giving it to average people and for strongly supporting local government. However, he also had a darker side.

Jackson was responsible for multiple attacks on Indian armies while he worked in the military, committed atrocities against Indian villages and led a major ethnic cleansing campaign called "The Trail of Tears." The Trail of Tears involved the forcible removal of 46,000 Indians, the largest removal in American history. Partly because of his policies to eliminate the Indians, Jackson was very popular during his presidency.

In many ways, Jackson was an impressive man. Born in 1767, he never had a school education. Instead, he taught himself the law during his teenage years and became a lawyer. Later, he became a very successful general in the US Army. During the War of 1812, with only 5,000 troops, he destroyed both the British and Creek Indians who were attacking New Orleans. This made him a hero for Americans. He added to his legend in 1818 by putting down a rebellion by the Creek Indian tribe. The Creeks had been attacking local whites and helping the British. Even though the Creeks seemed much stronger than Jackson's forces, Jackson crushed them.

After his victory Jackson performed extremely cruel atrocities to the defeated Creek Indians butchering them like animals. Jackson continued the atrocities afterwards. He burned Creek houses with people still trapped inside. His troops would treat prisoners with extreme cruelty and barbarity. With the Creek Indians destroyed, Jackson took more than 2,000,000 acres of their land in what is now Alabama.

Jackson also invaded the Seminole (an Indian tribe) territory in Florida after the Seminoles attacked neighboring white settlements. The Seminoles owned black slaves, however, they sometimes harbored fugitive slaves from white settlements. Jackson did not wait for permission from the government, invading and defeating the Seminoles by himself. He didn't treat the Seminoles any better than the Creek. He burned more than 100 houses and kidnapped hundreds of Seminole women and children to use as slaves.

Jackson became president in 1828. He was worried that Indian blood and culture would make the white race weak. He was worried that white American traditions and values would not survive with Indians around. As such, he made laws that destroyed Indian governments. As an example, he made a law stating that Indian leaders could never meet, except when they were selling land to white people. While Jackson's presidency had many successes, and he was very popular, he also killed and ethnically cleansed more Indians than any other president.

Resources	
For more information on Indian cultural tourism, visit http://traveltips.usatoday.com/vacations-indian-reservations-58153.html	
For more information on cultural appropriation of Native American traditions, visit http://www.mtv.com/news/1837578/why-you-should-not-wear-headdresses/	

#1

Imagine you were a Native American. Would you like or dislike William Penn?

Reasons to like William Penn	Reasons to dislike William Penn
1. 2. 3.	1. 2. 3.

#2

How should strong countries like Korea or Japan treat weak countries like Vietnam or Afghanistan?

#3

Americans loved both William Penn and Andrew Jackson. How can you explain this?

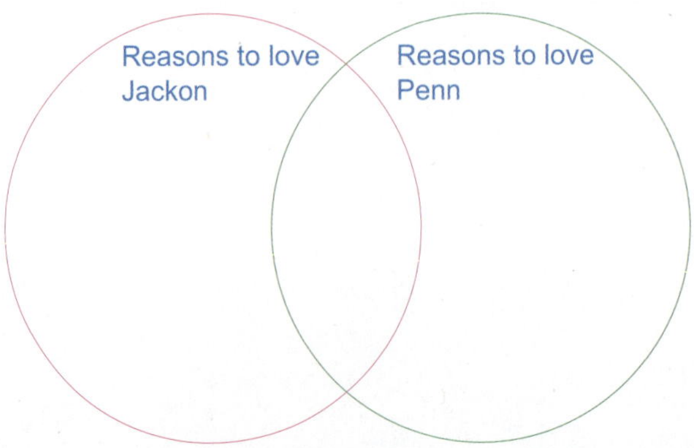

#4

Which leader is more Roman?

#5

Is it okay to erase "bad" cultures like ISIS or underdeveloped cultures like North Korea?

Good times to erase	Bad times to erase
1.	1.
2.	2.

08

Robert E. Lee and the American Civil War

Confederate General Robert E. Lee

Pre-reading vocabulary and phrases

plantation	a large farm, especially in a hot part of the world, on which a particular type of crop is grown
Confederacy	government of the southern states during the US Civil War
Union	the government of the northern states during the US Civil War
secession	the act of leaving an organization or government
reconciliation	a situation in which two people or groups of people become friendly again after they have argued
abolitionist	a person who supports ending slavery
pardon	an official decision to forgive someone who has committed a crime and allow them to be free

Visit the American South today and you might find a lot of anger against the North. Some Southerners will say that "all we want is to be left alone." Some of them will describe the North as a land of tyranny, where rich New Yorkers work to take away Southern freedoms.* A sizeable minority will remember all the thousands of men who died trying to make the South independent.

Some will describe Abraham Lincoln as scum. The South will rise again, some say. The South will one day escape from the evil United States and reunite under its old Confederate Flag. It will fight back against Northern civil rights organizations like the NAACP and ACLU and make a true Southern country where everyone is free. It will give everyone local control so that no terrible president can ever come down and destroy the South again.

In this new South, some believe, the people will become rich and prosperous. They are only poor and crime-ridden now, these people say, because the North oppresses them. Once the Northern interference and imperialism is removed, the South can become glorious.

The Confederate Flag. Some activists encourage people to burn these flags every September 12th.

Visit the American North and you can likewise hear a lot about the South. You will see some Northerners turn up their noses and describe Southerners as "white trash." You might hear the Confederates referred to as traitors and social cancer.*

Ask a Northerner about mistakes from the Civil War, and he might to say something like "we should have shot all the slave owners and destroyed the cities." Northerners commonly believe that "Southern pride" is just a code word for racism. A sizeable minority of Northerners will describe the South as that place where everything is primitive and broken. They will say that the South has horrible crime, poor education and poverty. A few will say "I'm tired of paying taxes to support Southern failure."

If you want to make an American angry, asking about the North and South is a pretty good strategy. But how did this anger and division start? What has locked Northern and Southern people in such an unhappy marriage? Let's explore the US Civil War and find out.

Before the Civil War, Northern states had illegalized slavery and switched to an industrial economy. Northern states favored central power, like William the Conqueror had, and divided power like in Magna Carta. Southern states, on the other hand, resisted industrial development and preferred to use slaves on giant farms.* They favored "states' rights" where individual states could overpower the central government. The disagreements on slavery and whether power should be with the central government or states eventually caused the Southern states to rebel in 1861.

The most important leader in the North was Abraham Lincoln and the most important leader in the South was a general named Robert E. Lee. This is the story of how Robert E. Lee, who didn't particularly like slavery and wanted the North and South to unite, ended up leading a rebellion against the United States.

Robert E. Lee was born to an aristocratic Virginia family in 1807. His family included politicians, plantation owners and businessmen. There were former presidents, Supreme Court judges, signers of the Declaration of Independence (an American document about freedom partly inspired by Magna Carta) and several war heroes among his ancestors. Lee's father, Henry Lee, had been a one of General George Washington's favorite military commanders.

When he was 18, Lee went to study at the famous military college, West Point. He was one of the finest students in the history of West Point and was known for his excellent understanding of artillery, infantry and cavalry. He later married one of George Washington's descendants and had seven children.

Lee left his family and slaves in Virginia to focus on his military career. He first became famous in 1846, when he led troops against Mexico in the Mexican War. The generals recognized Lee for exceptional brilliance and bravery and made him one of America's greatest heroes. Lee's commander said he was everything a soldier and American should try to be.

Afterwards, Lee retired and returned to his family and slaves. He tried to live as a manager, but was unhappy with the lifestyle. He jumped at the opportunity to rejoin the military in 1859. He was so desperate to escape from the civilian lifestyle that he took a very low position in Texas. However, it wasn't long before he had to fight against slaves rebelling against their slave masters. Because of his strategic brilliance and careful planning, Lee was able to end the rebellion in only one hour, with very few deaths. This improved his reputation even more.

The Civil War began in 1861 when the Southern states attacked the Northern-controlled Fort Sumter. Virginia, Lee's home state, aligned with the Southern rebels. President Lincoln actually offered control of the Northern Army to Lee, but he refused because Lee felt more loyal to his home state than he did to the United States. As such, Lee resigned from the military. Lee did not want to fight for the Confederacy either, and did not ultimately begin fighting until Virginia formally chose to join the Confederacy. Lee thought it was stupid to fight a war over slavery, but wanted to protect his neighbors and his state and so agreed to help the rebel army.

Group Project: State's rights take freedom away from weak people like racial and religious minorities. Is this a fair statement or not? Discuss with classmates.

In the early parts of the war, Lee won several important battles against the much stronger Northern forces. He took control of the Army of Northern Virginia and defeated a Northern invasion of Virginia. He also won important battles in Tennessee. His success was so great he decided to try an invasion of the North. This,

Lee hoped, would convince Lincoln to give up and accept the South's desire for secession.

This plan, however, ended in disaster. In a battle called Antietam, Lee barely escaped after losing 14,000 soldiers. Soon after, he faced another huge defeat in the battle of Gettysburg, where the North finally started to gain the advantage over the South. These two battles nearly destroyed Lee's army.

By 1864, the North had found a competent general named Ulysses S. Grant (previous Union generals had been very ineffective). With his greater resources and more plentiful soldiers, Grant was able to destroy many cities in the South. By 1865, it was clear the Confederacy could not win. Lee, ashamed and defeated, had to surrender to General Grant. He said this about the experience.

"I suppose there is nothing for me to do but go and see General Grant," he told an aide. "And I would rather die a thousand deaths."

While President Lincoln and General Grant could have executed Lee for treason, they instead pardoned him and allowed Lee to return to his family in Virginia. Lee spent the rest of his life working as the president of a small Virginia university and trying to help reconcile northern and southern citizens.

During the Civil War, Lee commanded the entire Southern army against the much larger, much better equipped Northern forces. While the Union won, it was mostly because of Lee's genius that the weaker, technologically primitive South wasn't immediately crushed. These days, Lee's reputation has become very complicated. Some Americans – mostly Northerners and black people - think of him as a racist and traitor, while many southern and white people think of him as a model of bravery.

Robert E. Lee: Slavery, Secession, and the Choice He Made

Adapted with permission from an article by Brooks D. Simpson

Southern General Robert E. Lee, seated center left, surrenders to Northern General Ulysses S. Grant, seated center right.]

It is important to discuss Lee's views on slavery, secession and the process by which he became the leader of the Confederacy. Lee's own thinking on these matters is easily accessible, especially through his writings. Lee's views on slavery were not terribly unusual for his time. They were a mixture of the "necessary evil" argument (which tended to emphasize the burdens slavery placed on white people) and the "positive good" argument (which tended to suggest that being enslaved benefited the black people). He did not believe in black equality, but he was not a defender of slavery. Lee did own slaves and he did discipline them, but he did not believe in an inevitable black inferiority to justify slavery. As he observed in an often-quoted letter:

(Note: We have re-written these quotes in simple, modern English. They are not exact quotations of Lee's original words.)

"In our enlightened times, I think you will have a hard time finding anyone who thinks slavery is a good thing. It is so evil on moral, institutional and political levels that I think it's useless to spend more time talking about its disadvantages. I think it is worse for white people than for black people and while my feelings are stronger for the black slaves, my concern is stronger for the white people. This is because the blacks are much better off living in the US as slaves than they would be living freely in Africa. If they were still in Africa, they would be morally, socially and physically suffering much more. They need the painful process of slavery to teach them civilization and proper morality and I hope this process leads them to better accomplishments and more happiness in the future. Only God knows how long they will require subjugation until this process is complete."

Yet it is also important to recall what he wrote this in 1865:

"When I think of the relationship between slaves and masters and consider the laws maintaining humane treatment of slaves, I think that slavery is the best option for our times. I would disagree with any attempt to suddenly get rid of slavery unless it was necessary to prevent an even worse catastrophe for both blacks and whites."

These words are carefully chosen. Lee was not an anti-slavery hero, but he was also not arguing for infinite black subjugation. His position was, for the time, moderate.

Lee held abolitionists and anti-slavery critics primarily responsible for the troubling debate over slavery and the beginnings of the Civil War. He reserved his harshest words for anti-slavery activists, although he complained about the behavior of Deep South secessionists in 1860-61, including their "selfish, dictatorial bearing." Lee also had little patience with the elaborate philosophical arguments of the secessionists, simply acknowledging that "secession is nothing but revolution." That said, he mostly blamed the North. "The South, in my opinion, has been aggrieved by the acts of the North."

If he dismissed the theory of secession as nonsense, however, Lee took the North and South crisis quite seriously. He said "a Union that can only be maintained by swords and bayonets (with the power of northern armies), and in which strife and civil war are to replace brotherly love and kindness, has no charm for me."

That statement is essential to understanding Lee's loyalty. As he put it, "If the Union is dissolved, and the Government disrupted, I shall return to my native State and share the miseries of my people, and save in defense will draw my sword on none."

In other words, he didn't want to fight for either the North or South, but would only fight if Virginia was attacked.

아브라함 링컨과 로버트 E. 리는 실제로 매우 유사한 인물이었습니다. 둘 중 누구도 미국의 남북전쟁을 원하지 않았고, 둘 다 노예제도가 큰 전쟁을 통하지 않고 점차적으로 사라지길 바랐습니다. 노예제도를 합법화하고 싶어하지 않은 것이 이 둘의 공통된 점이었습니다. 링컨은 남쪽이 반역하기 전 이미 노예제도를 금지하였습니다. 그들은 모두 남부의 분리 독립이론이 말도 안 된다고 생각하였습니다. 하지만 그들 사이에도 의견 차이가 있었는데 그것은 바로 충성심의 「방향」에 있었습니다. 링컨은 국가가 주(州)보다 더 중요하다고 생각하였습니다. 반면에 로버트 E. 리 장군은 주(州)가 국가보다 더 중요하다고 생각했습니다. 링컨과 로버트 E. 리 장군의 의견 불일치는 영미권 역사에서 매우 중요한 사건입니다. 외국인을 포함 또는 제외하는 것에 대한 의견 차이 같은 문제와 함께 이러한 문제들은 1000년 이상 영미문화를 형성하는데 뿌리 깊게 적용됐습니다.

Resources	
For a southern perspective on the Civil War, visit https://www.boundless.com/u-s-history/textbooks/boundless-u-s-history-textbook/reconstruction-1865-1877-19/the-aftermath-of-the-war-138/devastation-in-the-south-733-6732/	
For an example of northern animosity towards pro-Confederate southerners, visit http://www.huffingtonpost.com/john-e-price/yes-youre-a-racist----and-a-traitor_b_7640654.html	
For more information on the slave economy, visit http://freakonomics.com/2011/06/07/why-does-the-south-still-commemorate-the-civil-war-but-not-the-north-bring-your-questions-for-historian-peter-coclanis/	

#1

Imagine two scenarios. In the 1st scenario, you are a white southerner. In the 2nd scenario, you are a black northerner. How would you feel about Robert E. Lee's opinion on slavery?

Scenario #1	Scenario #2
1. 2. 3.	1. 2. 3.

#2

Robert E. Lee was more loyal to his state than his country. Are you more loyal to your province or your country? Why?

#3

How can northern and southern Americans reconcile? Research East and West Germany.(Optional: Rwanda has reconciled very effectively after the 1991 Rwandan Civil War. If you prefer, you can research Rwanda instead of Germany.) Present your findings.

#4

Compare Robert E Lee with William the Conqueror and the Romans.

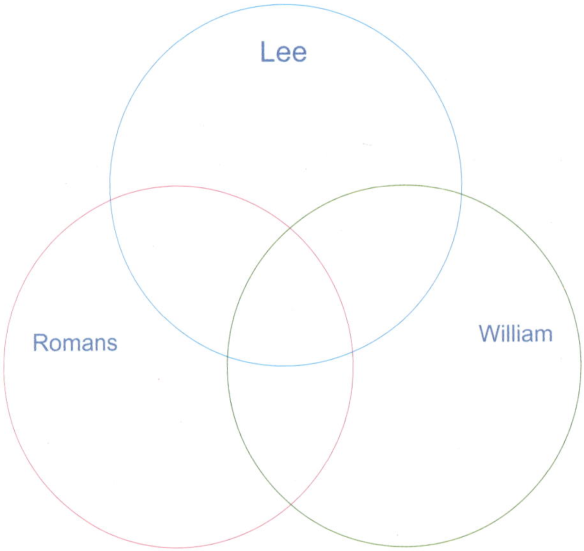

#5

The former president of Korea, Park Jung-Hee, had a problem called "regionalism". Can the American Civil War offer any lessons about Korean regionalism?

Insights from the US Civil War	Insights from other sources (Russia, China, etc.)
1.	1.
2.	2.
3.	3.
4.	4.
5.	5.

09

Cecil Rhodes and Imperialism

Cecil Rhodes, the founder of Rhodesia and a famous imperialist.

Pre-reading vocabulary and phrases

fiefdom	an area or type of activity that is controlled by someone
mining claim	a statement of ownership for a mine
conventional wisdom	typical and traditional beliefs of a culture or group
stage a coup	a group of people suddenly taking control of a country by using force

본 책의 저자를 포함한 현대의 서양인들은 사회 진화론을 믿지 않습니다. 하지만 1800년대 후반과 1900년대 초반은 제국주의의 전성기였습니다. 당시에는 대부분의 사람들이 사회 진화론이라는 이론을 믿었습니다. 사회 진화론에 따르면 유럽 국가들이 번성한 이유는 유럽인들이 다른 인종들보다 우수한 인종이었기 때문이라고합니다. 구한 말 조선 같은 경우는 열강들에 의해 희생당하는 약소국가이었는데 이 또한 사회 진화론자들은 인종의 우 · 열에서 그 이유를 찾고자 했습니다.

최악의 사회 진화론자들로 평가받는 이들은 벨기에의 레오폴드 왕과 나치독일의 아돌프 히틀러 같은 역사적 인물들입니다. 이 사람들은 상대적으로 강한 인종들이 다른 "보다 열등한" 인종들을 동물과 같이 이용할 수 있다고 믿었습니다. 하지만 모든 사회 진화론자들이 이렇게 잔인했던건 아닙니다. 미합중국 26대 대통령 테디 루스벨트 (다음장에서 소개될 인물)와 저명한 소설가 러디어드 키플링 같은 인물은 백인들이 우수한 문화를 가졌으며 이러한 문화를 상대적으로 열등한 문화를 가진 민족들에게 가르치는 것이 그들이 더 번성하고, 부유해지도록 "도와 주는 방법"이라고 믿었습니다. 세실 로즈 역시 확실한 사회 진화론자였습니다. 세실로즈가 레오폴드 왕과 아돌프 히틀러 같은 잔인한 사회 진화론자이었는지 아니면 테디 루스벨트와 키플링 같은 "문화전용" 사회 다원주의자이었는지에 대한 평가는 열린 질문형식입니다. 아프리카에서의 제국주의에 대한 그의 논지를 중점으로 다음을 읽어보시기 바랍니다.

여기에서 잠깐 "세실 로즈"에 의해 창립된 로즈 장학재단에 대해 잠시 소개 하겠습니다. 우리나라 정부가 세계의 인재들에게 한국에서의 공부 기회를 제공하는 장학재단을 GKS라고 합니다. 이러한 국비 장학금 제도로 미국에는 Fulbright Program, 일본에는 문부성 장학금 그리고 영국에는 로즈 장학금제도가 있습니다. 이 로즈 장학금이 본 단원에서 소개할 세실 로즈에 의해 창립되어 지금까지도 영국 국비 장학금 제도로 운영되고 있습니다.

The GSK(Global Scholarship in Korea) program is similar to the scholarship named after Cecil Rhodes, the Rhodes Scholarship. The reason the English national scholarship program is named after Rhodes is because Cecil Rhodes created an enormous fund big enough to support the best English students for hundreds of years.

To a British person, or an American especially, one of the strangest things a Korean person can talk about is "the Korean race." When a Korean person talks about the Korean race, it sounds very old fashioned, very odd and vaguely racist. One reason for this is that, not very long ago, protecting the white race was an important goal for British and American people. This desire caused a lot of problems and many modern Americans and British people are ashamed of it.

To make up for this shame, many British and American people today try to live "color-blind" lives.* This means they want to ignore all racial differences and treat everyone like they are the same. "Color-blindness" has made it possible to embrace interracial marriages. In fact, many British and American people think that mixed-race babies are better looking and healthier than babies from single-race families. They encourage young people to experience as many different cultures as possible because they think diversity makes society stronger. Many of the foreign teachers you've had in Korea likely came to Korea because they wanted to use their color-blind ideals.

1

2

3

4

5

6

7

8

Mixed race celebrities:

1. Actress Halle Berry is German, English and African.

2. Basketball star Blake Griffin's mother is Caucasian and his father is Haitian.

3. Matrix actor Keanu Reeves is Native Hawaiian, Chinese and English.

4. Prison Break star Wentworth Miller is Lebanese, Native American, African, Swedish and Russian.

5. Star football player Hines Ward's mother is Korean and his father is African American.

6. Actress Jessica Alba's ancestors were Mexican, French and Dutch.

7. Singer Beyonce Knowles is African, Native American and French.

8. Former US President Barack Obama's mother is English and his father is Kenyan.

This could not be more different from how Americans and British people used to think about mixed-raced people. A child whose father was black and mother was white would have been rejected by both white and black communities only 50 years ago. In many states, interracial marriage was illegal. When couples ignored the stigma against interracial couples, communities would sometimes kill the man.

Many of the reasons for protecting races came from an idea called Social Darwinism. While this idea is no longer popular, it was very important in shaping Britain and the United States, particularly regarding imperialism. There are very few examples of Social Darwinism better than Cecil Rhodes.

Cecil Rhodes stepping on all of Africa

Cecil Rhodes wrote his "Confession of Faith" when he was 23. It defined his vision for the future, his goal in life. What's most incredible about this extremely ambitious document is that Rhodes, while he didn't conquer the world, did come close to achieving these goals. He was never a king or president, but that didn't stop him from making Southern Africa into his personal fiefdom. He didn't unite the Anglo Saxon race, but he did fill Africa with Union Jacks (the British flag) and white, British settlers.

"Why should we not form a secret society with but one object, the furtherance of the British Empire and the bringing of the whole world under British rule, for the recovery of the United States, for making the Anglo Saxon race but one Empire? What a dream, but yet it is probably (sic), *it is possible."*

-Cecil Rhodes

Rhodes became rich when he was very young. He was a skilled miner and shrewd businessman. When he was 17, his brother gave him three diamond mines in Southern Africa. When the other miners thought the diamonds had run out, Rhodes bought all of their mines for very little money. He was gambling that the other miners were all wrong and, ultimately, he was correct. This sort of bold decision making would become a hallmark with Rhodes.

Rhodes' mines grew stronger and richer and more profitable. By 1888, with a combination of intimidation, business savvy and luck, he bought most of the rest of the Kimberly Mines. This created a company called "Rhodes De Beers Consolidated Mines." While De Beers is huge today, in 1888, it was so large it controlled 90% of the world's diamond production. Additionally, Rhodes had other successes in gold mines, becoming one of the richest people in world history.

However, wealth was never the end goal for Rhodes. Like he said in the Confession of Faith, he wanted to fix the entire world by controlling it with white Englishmen. In 1881, he became a member of the Parliament in Colonial Southern Africa. He used this power to take much more land from the native, African people. This quote illustrates Rhodes' attitude about imperialism.

"Africa is still lying ready for us. It is our duty to take it."

During the 1890's, his political power grew and he used his company to steal land from several local African chiefs. This gave him control of more mines and even more wealth. By 1896, he had crushed the last resistance and renamed the territory Rhodesia, in his own honor. He gave the new country to the Queen of England as a present.

Rhodes continued having success until he attacked the Boers (mostly the descendants of immigrant farmers from Holland). The Boers had discovered a rich area for mining gold and Rhodes wanted to control it. Rhodes' plan was to make a coup where policemen loyal to Rhodes would go to the Boer lands and support rebels. Unfortunately for Rhodes, this plan ended in disaster. The Boers easily caught the policemen and arrested them. The rebels, who were helping Rhodes, were also quickly destroyed. This failed coup embarrassed Rhodes so much he had to quit politics.

When Rhodes died, his legacy was complicated. While he could be greedy and immoral, he was also thought of as a great patriot. While he could act like a thief and followed racist ideals, he also accomplished his goal to make more of the world a home for white English people.

Discussion topic: Most powerful countries have patriotic heroes like Rhodes. Andrew Jackson is a patriotic hero in America. Toyotomi Hideyoshi is a patriotic hero in Japan. Josef Stalin is a patriotic hero in parts of Russia. Why do so many patriotic heroes remain heroes after doing terrible things?

Confession of Faith

Cecil Rhodes

(This essay has been copied exactly from Cecil Rhodes' original, including grammatical and spelling errors.)

청색으로 쓰여진 문서는 "신앙고백"의 원본입니다. 굵은 글로 쓰여진 문서 역시 같은 내용을 포함하고 있지만 이 책의 저자들에 의해 간편화 된 문서입니다.

People often wonder what makes a good life. Some people decide it is a happy marriage, some decide it is wealth. Regardless, he will work the rest of his life to achieve this goal. I decided the best goal was to become useful to my country.

When I asked myself how I could be most useful to my country, I decided that we English did not have enough land, that we were not sufficiently numerous. If we had America, for example, there would be millions more Englishmen living.

I believe that white Englishmen are the finest race in the world. If more of the world was inhabited by white Englishmen, it would be far better for humans in general. Imagine how much better it would be if we took countries from lesser races and ruled them with white Englishmen. How much better will countries become when we control them?

Every acre of land we control means we have space for more white Englishmen. Further, if white Englishmen control the entire world, it would be the end of all war. For example, if we had not lost America, I believe we could have stopped the Russian-Turkish war by merely refusing money and supplies.

We could have so much power if we organized. Even the Jesuits (a catholic sect) were able to control large areas with their organization and they had bad leadership.

I look at a group like the Free Masons (a secret social club) and I see their wealth and power. They could accomplish so much if only they had one, focused goal.

Here's my great idea, why don't we make a secret society that does nothing but expand the British Empire? Why don't we try to bring the whole uncivilized world under the control of Britain and re-conquer America?

Imagine how much better Americans would be if they had the civilizing influence of Britain. How much stronger their country would be if there had been more Englishmen controlling their savage impulses and populating their country?

Wouldn't the Americans be healthier and stronger without the inferior Irish and Germans dragging them down with dirty blood of lesser races?

It is just because of one or two English stupid politicians that America is not currently a part of Britain. Doesn't this make you mad? Don't you want to just kill somebody? I want to kill somebody when I think of these stupid politicians.

No good English father would ever want his son to emigrate to a country not controlled by Britain. That would be horrible, it is better to be poor under the British flag than rich under a foreign flag.

Think of Australia (at that time an English colony). If the French had colonized Australia, there would be several million fewer white Englishmen in the world, and the English people in Australia are our future.

Africa is still empty, though. It is open for us to take. It is not just an opportunity, it is our duty to take every piece of land that we can because that means we can have more white Englishmen. Since white Englishmen are the best race in the world, having more of them means the entire world becomes more human and more honorable.
Discussion topic: There were millions of black Africans in Africa. Why does Rhodes say Africa is empty?

Original Text:

It often strikes a man to inquire what is the chief good in life; to one the thought comes that it is a happy marriage, to another great wealth, and as each seizes on his idea, for that he more or less works for the rest of his existence. To myself thinking over the same question the wish came to render myself useful to my country.

I then asked myself how could I and after reviewing the various methods I have felt that at the present day we are actually limiting our children and perhaps bringing into the world half the human beings we might owing to the lack of country for them to inhabit that if we had retained America there would at this moment be millions more of English living.

I contend that we are the finest race in the world and that the more of the world we inhabit the better it is for the human race. Just fancy those parts that are at present inhabited by the most despicable specimens of human beings what an alteration there would be if they were brought under Anglo-Saxon influence, look again at the extra employment a new country added to our dominions gives.

I contend that every acre added to our territory means in the future birth to some more of the English race who otherwise would not be brought into existence. Added to this the absorption of the greater portion of the world under our rule simply means the end of all wars, at this moment had we not lost America I believe we could have stopped the Russian-Turkish war by merely refusing money and supplies.

Having these ideas what scheme could we think of to forward this object. I look into history and I read the story of the Jesuits I see what they were able to do in a bad cause and I might say under bad leaders.

At the present day I become a member of the Masonic order I see the wealth and power they possess the influence they hold and I think over their ceremonies and I wonder that a large body of men can devote themselves to what at times appear the most ridiculous and absurd rites without an object and without an end.

The idea gleaming and dancing before ones eyes like a will-of-the-wisp at last frames itself into a plan. Why should we not form a secret society with but one object the furtherance of the British Empire and the bringing of the whole uncivilised world under

British rule for the recovery of the United States for the making the Anglo-Saxon race but one Empire. What a dream, but yet it is probable, it is possible.

I once heard it argued by a fellow in my own college, I am sorry to own it by an Englishman, that it was good thing for us that we have lost the United States. There are some subjects on which there can be no arguments, and to an Englishman this is one of them, but even from an American's point of view, just picture what they have lost, look at their government, are not the frauds that yearly come before the public view a disgrace to any country and especially their's which is the finest in the world. Would they have occurred had they remained under English rule great as they have become how infinitely greater they would have been with the softening and elevating influences of English rule, think of those countless 000's of Englishmen that during the last 100 years would have crossed the Atlantic and settled and populated the United States.

Would they have not made without any prejudice a finer country of it than the low class Irish and German emigrants?

All this we have lost and that country loses owing to whom? Owing to two or three ignorant pig-headed statesmen of the last century, at their door lies the blame. Do you ever feel mad? do you ever feel murderous. I think I do with those men.

I bring facts to prove my assertion. Does an English father when his sons wish to emigrate ever think of suggesting emigration to a country under another flag, never—it would seem a disgrace to suggest such a thing I think that we all think that poverty is better under our own flag than wealth under a foreign one.

Put your mind into another train of thought. Fancy Australia discovered and colonized under the French flag, what would it mean merely several millions of English unborn that at present exist we learn from the past and to form our future. We learn from having lost to cling to what we possess. We know the size of the world we know the total extent.

Africa is still lying ready for us it is our duty to take it. It is our duty to seize every opportunity of acquiring more territory and we should keep this one idea steadily before our eyes that more territory simply means more of the Anglo-Saxon race more of the best the most human, most honorable race the world possesses.

Resources

For more information on "color blindness," visit http://thesocietypages.org/specials/colorblindness-vs-race-consciousness/	
For more information on the slave economy, visit https://www.boundless.com/u-s-history/textbooks/boundless-u-s-history-textbook/race-empire-and-culture-in-the-gilded-age-1870-1900-21/culture-in-the-gilded-age-157/social-darwinism-in-america-846-883	

#1

Japan believed in imperialism in the late 19th century until 1945. How did Japanese imperialism affect Korea?

1. One positive change	1. One negative change
2. Original situation	
3. How was it changed?	
4. Why was it changed?	

#2

Now choose a different country that experienced imperialism. Repeat the steps for question # 1. Country name:_____(Ex. Cuba)______________

1. One positive change	1. One negative change
2. Original situation	
3. How was it changed?	
4. Why was it changed?	

#3

How should rich countries, like Britain or South Korea, treat poor countries, like the Philippines or Pakistan?

#4

Do you prefer to be rich in a foreign country or poor in Korea?

	Poor in Korea	Rich overseas
Advantages		
Disadvantages		

#5

America has some imperialism in its history. The UK has a huge amount of imperialism in its history. Did imperialism help the US and England develop?

10

Theodore Roosevelt and Manliness

President Theodore Roosevelt posing in his Rough Rider's uniform.

Pre-reading vocabulary and phrases

win office	to be elected
in his/her own right	by one's own merit
without flinching	without showing fear
commercial interest	a business
run from a fight	to avoid conflict, usually because of cowardice

Ben first came to Korea in 2008. At the time, Big Bang was extremely popular and the band members appeared in many TV advertisements, on buses and in magazines. Because he had very little experience with Korean culture at the time, he judged the Big Bang members by his American standards. When he used his American standards of manliness to look at the Big Bang members, to examine their clothes, hair styles and actions, he assumed they were all homosexuals.

Several of Young-Joo and Ben's male, Korean students had trouble when they traveled to the US, England or Canada. Because they dressed in styles fashionable for young Korean men, locals in the US, England or Canada thought they were gay. One of Ben's students said "when I got to Canada, I wasn't popular with the girls, but I was very popular with gay guys."

Big Bang, demonstrating that a Korean man's fashionable styles are very different from American or English fashionable styles.

Similarly, Ben's new Korean friends were confused with his notions of manliness. He heard questions like "why do American and British men have ugly mustaches and beards? "Why do Americans and British men want to look so huge and muscular? Don't they know it makes them look like animals and not people? Why don't they want to look cute, like Korean men?"

For young American and English men, ideas of manly style mostly center around ideas of strength, independence and toughness. An American man who can kill a deer, build a car engine and pull a piece of glass from his foot without crying is very impressive in America. A British man who plays rugby, carves a boat out of wood and ignores broken fingers will almost certainly be admired by other men and desired by women. American and English men often brag about scars and show off their old injuries.*

On the other hand, young Korean men build their styles around ideas of sensitivity and cuteness. A Korean man who understands what types of flowers women like best is very admirable. If he has white, smooth skin and delicate hands, that' s even better. If a Korean man is described as "pretty like a flower," that's a good thing. Describe an American man as "pretty like a flower" and you will almost certainly hurt his feelings.*

While it's very difficult to choose one event that created British and American ideals of manliness, we can trace many of them back to the late 19th and early 20th centuries. It's hard to think of a better manly man from this time than former US President Theodore Roosevelt.

Many young American or English men want to look something like American fighter Shane Carwin, American soldier Pat Tillman or British explorer Bear Grylls

Theodore Roosevelt was the 26th US President. While he was a very effective president – breaking economic monopolies, making education a right for all children, fighting corruption, making the first environmental protections and turning the United States into a powerful naval nation – he is better known for his manliness.

While he was born rich, Roosevelt was also a very sick and weak child. This filled him with an intense shame. When he was sick, he would read about the great warriors and leaders of the past and yearn to join their ranks. To do this, he spent his youth pursuing what he called "the strenuous life." He became a boxer, a hunter of dangerous animals and a cowboy. By the time he graduated from Harvard University (the other students thought Roosevelt "eccentric and odd") he had become a physically strong and courageous man.

He won office as the police commissioner in New York and became famous for destroying corrupt police and political organizations. However, when the US went to war with Spain in 1898, Roosevelt wanted to fight so bad that he resigned his job as police commissioner and joined the military. The US offered him a position as admiral (the navy equivalent of general), but he refused. Roosevelt did not want power that he had not earned. Instead, he became a minor officer.

The group he led came to be known as the "Rough Riders." These were 560 men chosen by Roosevelt personally. They were the best western cowboys, the strongest Indian warriors, most experienced black soldiers, finest eastern athletes and the brightest scholars. They all wanted to earn glory in battle. During the war, this group became famous for their extreme bravery and Roosevelt became famous for his toughness.

He would not ride a horse while his men had to walk. Neither would he ask any soldier to do something he would not also do – he would encourage his men to attack by standing up in the open air while the enemy shot at him. Once, when he led a charge, only five of the other soldiers heard him. Roosevelt ran several hundred meters almost by himself while attacking the enemy before he realized that only two soldiers were with him. He turned around, gathered more men, and attacked again, this time successfully. As a result, Roosevelt won the highest possible military award, the Medal of Honor.

After his presidency, Roosevelt joined with Brazillian explorer Candido Rondon, an extremely tough and brave man in his own right, on a scientific expedition to the unmapped "River of Doubt" in the Amazon rainforest. Roosevelt caught malaria, crushed a bone in his leg and survived attacks from cannibal Indians, but still didn't want to be treated any different from the common men and servants traveling with him. The expedition resulted in the first mapping of an important river in the Amazon basin, the discovery of several new species of animal and the deaths of three explorers.

By the time he died five years later, Roosevelt, with his bravery, toughness and reluctance to put himself above others, had become a model for manliness in the United States and the West in general.

Roles for Men

In chapter six we discussed the three tropes that tend to describe powerful women. In the Anglo-sphere, at least, there are a lot more tropes that can apply to powerful men. A male Femme Fatale, for example, would just be a handsome guy with lots of girlfriends. It would be very impractical to list all of these possible roles, so we are instead going to talk about just a few of the most important.

The bully likes to use his power and strength, but only against weaker people.

The Bully –Just like the femme fatale is dangerous due to her extreme and dangerous femininity, the bully is dangerous because his masculinity is exaggerated and perverted. The bully is aggressive, but only to people weaker than himself. He is often very showy and he often brags, but his confidence is fake.

The bully is an undesirable type for Anglo-American men because he is perceived as having fake manliness. After all, the point of a man in Anglo-American mythology is to lead and protect others. That's hard to do if the man only leads and protects when things are safe.

Examples of the bully in real life include a lot of cruel but cowardly people like Roman Emperor Nero, Joseon king Yeonsangun and Fred Phelps, an American activist who attacks and criticizes grieving families at funerals.

The Sissy–A sissy is a weak or effeminate man who allows others to manipulate or victimize him. In the same sense that a Nurse Ratched is distorted and repulsive womanhood, the sissy is a gross distortion of masculinity. A man who cannot protect himself or his family would be considered a sissy along with any man who is too afraid of getting hurt. This comes from the idea that a man should be brave, yes, but also from the idea that a man should be willing to die or suffer for the sake of women and children.

One of the most powerful concepts in gender roles is the idea of victimization. Women are allowed to be victims and, in some cases, even encouraged to embrace the role of passive victim. Men, on the other hand, are often considered failures or embarrassments if they allow others to victimize them. After all, men are supposed to be in control of themselves and their situations. A sissy is thus anathema to Anglo American ideals of masculinity.

Examples of sissies include weak, ineffective and easily manipulated men like Emperor Hirohito of Japan, the disastrous Roman emperor Honorius and the extremely soft King Edward VIII of England.

The Cultured Bruiser –Like the mother to her country, the cultured bruiser is considered the pinnacle of his gender. A cultured bruiser is calm, thoughtful and well educated. He is very likely to understand Greek theatre and enjoy fine wines. However, this does not stop him from being physically strong, courageous and imposing. He might read Dante in the morning and then spend the evening boxing or hunting in the forest.Even if he becomes sick or gets old, the cultured bruiser commands respect with his toughness and composure.

Cultured Bruisers like Simon Bolivar are brave, sophisticated and wise.

Where the bully feels the need to show off his masculinity, a cultured bruiser is so confident in his manliness that he doesn't need to make displays. Where the sissy is constantly being taken advantage of and manipulated, the Cultured Bruiser sees through the schemes and attacks of his enemies and protects the people following him from harm.

Theodore Roosevelt, who was at different points in his life a historian, an Amazonian explorer, one of the first environmentalists, a cowboy, a soldier and a politician, is an excellent example of the vultured bruiser in real life. Other examples of real life cultured bruisers include men like the Roman philosopher king Marcus Aurelius, Taizhong, co-founder of the Tang Dynasty, Korean Admiral Yi Soon-shin and Kiwi engineer, racing driver and inventor Bruce McLaren.

The Strenuous Life

Theodore Roosevelt, 1899

Roosevelt poses with Brazilian explorer Candido Rondon. The two men were exploring the River of Doubt in the Amazon when this photo was taken.

This is a simplified version of the original speech:

To all the people of Illinois, where the great president Abraham Lincoln and the great general Ulysses S. Grant came from, I want to promote not a life of luxury but the strenuous life. I want you to embrace hard work, difficult challenges and the willingness to fight. To fight, work hard and try for amazing goals is far better than living in quiet, lazy safety.

An ignoble, easy life of peace can come from a lack of ambition. This is a shameful thing for both individuals and nations. What good father would teach his son that the highest goal should be ease? The men of Chicago have made this city great because they reject such lessons. If you are rich, you should raise your sons so that they use their free time in science, literature, art, exploration or historical work. This is the sort of thing that brings a nation honor, not lazy comfort.

It is much better to try great things, to have amazing triumphs and great failures than to be like the gray people who feel neither joy nor suffering. They know neither victory nor defeat. If during the Civil War the men who loved the Union (the Northern States) had believed peace was the greatest priority, that war and fighting were always bad, they could have saved thousands of lives. They could have saved millions of dollars and stopped the suffering for thousands of families. They could have done this simply by giving up. But if we had done so, we would have shown the rest of the world how weak we were, and that we are unworthy to stand with the great countries. Thank God that we did not accept this ignoble peace. We faced sadness and despair, endured strife and did not flinch. In the end, we freed the slaves, reunited the nation and raised the American Republic to greater heights.

We can't be isolationists like China, which is content to rot away little by little, happy with its easy life and looking only to make money. We have to take interest in foreign countries. We have to embrace risk and hard work because, if we don't, we'll end up like China – a weak country beaten by more manly nations. If we want to be great, we need to try and be benevolently involved in the affairs of many nations. (See note at the end of this speech.)

Timid men, lazy men, men who are unpatriotic, over-civilized or have lost the will to fight, stupid men and men without ambition – these men fear the strenuous life. They believe in quiet safety, even as that quiet safety sucks the strength from their countries and bodies. They care only about greed, only commercial interests. Commercial interests are important, but they are just one part of what makes a nation great.

The cowards afraid to fight are responsible for a lot of bloodshed in the Philippines. These fake humanitarians asked primitive people to fight in a war they could never win and, as such, got a lot of natives and Americans killed when the situation turned bad.

We are just beginning the 20th century and I hope that, instead of ignoble ease, we adopt the strenuous life. If we are idle, then the men of other countries will surpass us and win the world. We must face life without fear, do our duties in the rest of the world and use pragmatism. We must never run from a fight or let cowardice control our actions. The only way to have a great nation is through hard work and danger.

Original Text

In speaking to you, men of the greatest city of the West, men of the State which gave to the country Lincoln and Grant, men who pre-eminently and distinctly embody all that is most American in the American character, I wish to preach, not the doctrine of ignoble ease, but the doctrine of the strenuous life, the life of toil and effort, of labor and strife; to preach that highest form of success which comes, not to the man who desires mere easy peace, but to the man who does not shrink from danger, from hardship, or from bitter toil, and who out of these wins the splendid ultimate triumph.

A life of ignoble ease, a life of that peace which springs merely from lack either of desire or of power to strive after great things, is as little worthy of a nation as of an individual. I ask only that what every self-respecting American demands from himself and from his sons shall be demanded of the American nation as a whole. Who among you would teach your boys that ease, that peace, is to be the first consideration in their eyes-to be the ultimate goal after which they strive? You men of Chicago have made this city great, you men of Illinois have done your share, and more than your share, in making America great, because you neither preach nor practice such a doctrine. You work yourselves, and you bring up your sons to work. If you are rich and are worth your salt, you will teach your sons that though they may have leisure, it is not to be spent in idleness; for wisely used leisure merely means that those who possess it, being free from the necessity of working for their livelihood, are all the more bound to carry on some kind of non-remunerative work in science, in letters, in art, in exploration, in historical research-work of the type we most need in this country, the successful carrying out of which reflects most honor upon the nation.

Far better it is to dare mighty things, to win glorious triumphs, even though checkered by failure, than to take rank with those poor spirits who neither enjoy much nor suffer much, because they live in the gray twilight that knows not victory nor defeat. If in 1861 (the American Civil War) *the men who loved the Union had believed that peace was the end of all things, and war and strife the worst of all things, and had acted up to their belief, we would have saved hundreds of thousands of lives, we would have saved hundreds of millions of dollars. Moreover, besides saving all the blood and treasure we then lavished, we would have prevented the heartbreak of many women, the dissolution of many homes, and we would have spared the country those months of gloom and shame when it seemed as if our armies marched only to defeat. We could have avoided all this suffering simply by shrinking from strife. And if we had thus avoided it, we would have shown that we were weaklings, and that we were unfit to stand among the great nations of the earth. Thank God that the ignoble counsels of peace were rejected; that the suffering and loss, the blackness of sorrow and despair, were unflinchingly faced, and the years of strife endured; for in the end the slave was freed, the Union restored, and the mighty American republic placed once more as a helmeted queen among nations.*

We cannot, if we would, play the part of China, and be content to rot by inches in ignoble ease within our borders, taking no interest in what goes on beyond them, sunk in a scrambling commercialism; heedless of the higher life, the life of aspiration, of toil and risk, busying ourselves only with the wants of our bodies for the day, until suddenly we should find, beyond a shadow of question, what China has already found, that in this world the nation that has trained itself to a career of unwarlike and isolated ease is bound, in the end, to go down before other nations which have not lost the manly and adventurous qualities. If we are to be a really great people, we must strive in good faith to play a great part in the world.

The timid man, the lazy man, the man who distrusts his country, the over-civilized man, who has lost the great fighting, masterful virtues, the ignorant man, and the man of dull mind, whose soul is incapable of feeling the mighty lift that thrills "stern men with empires in their brains"-all these, of course, shrink from seeing the nation undertake its new duties. These are the men who fear the strenuous life, who fear the only national life which is really worth leading. They believe in that cloistered life which saps the hardy virtues in a nation, as it saps them in the individual; or else they are wedded to that base spirit of gain and greed which recognizes in commercialism the be-all and end-all of national life, instead of realizing that, though an indispensable element, it is, after all, but one of the many elements that go to make up true national greatness.

So, at the present hour, no small share of the responsibility for the blood shed in the Philippines, the blood of our brothers, and the blood of their wild and ignorant foes, lies at the thresholds of those who so long delayed the adoption of the treaty of peace, and of those who by their worse than foolish words deliberately invited a savage people to plunge into a war fraught with sure disaster for them – a war, too, in which our own brave men who follow the flag must pay with their blood for the silly, mock humanitarianism of the prattlers who sit at home in peace.

I preach to you, then, my countrymen, that our country calls not for the life of ease but for the life of strenuous endeavor. The twentieth century looms before us big with the fate of many nations. If we stand idly by, if we seek merely swollen, slothful ease and ignoble peace, if we shrink from the hard contests where men must win at hazard of their lives and at the risk of all they hold dear, then the bolder and stronger peoples will pass us by, and will win for themselves the domination of the world. Let us therefore boldly face the life of strife, resolute to do our duty well and manfully; resolute to uphold righteousness by deed and by word; resolute to be both honest and brave, to serve high ideals, yet to use practical methods. Above all, let us shrink from no strife, moral or physical, within or without the nation, provided we are certain that the strife is justified, for it is only through strife, through hard and dangerous endeavor, that we shall ultimately win the goal of true national greatness.

1899년 루즈벨트대통령의 연설이 만들어졌을 시기에, 중국은 조선과 같이 고립주의를 추구하고, 약하고 부패한 국가였습니다. 중국의 지도자들은 외세의 영향을 차단하기 위한 시도를 했지만 중국은 기술력이 당시 서구에 비해 발달하지 못하여 유럽과 일본의 제국주의자들로부터 자국의 땅을 지켜내지 못했습니다. 중국이 그 당시에 얼마나 약소 국가였는지 보여주는 사례로 아편전쟁과 의화단 운동을 읽어 보십시오.

Resources	
For more information on Western masculinity and Eastern masculinity, visit http://theconversation.com/un-designing-masculinities-k-pop-and-the-new-global-man-22335	
For more information on the social meaning of masculinity in the West, visit http://www.lltjournal.ca/index.php/llt/article/viewFile/4716/5589	

#1

	Your opinion	Roosevelt's opinion
Manliness		
Peace		
Struggle		
Fighting		

#2

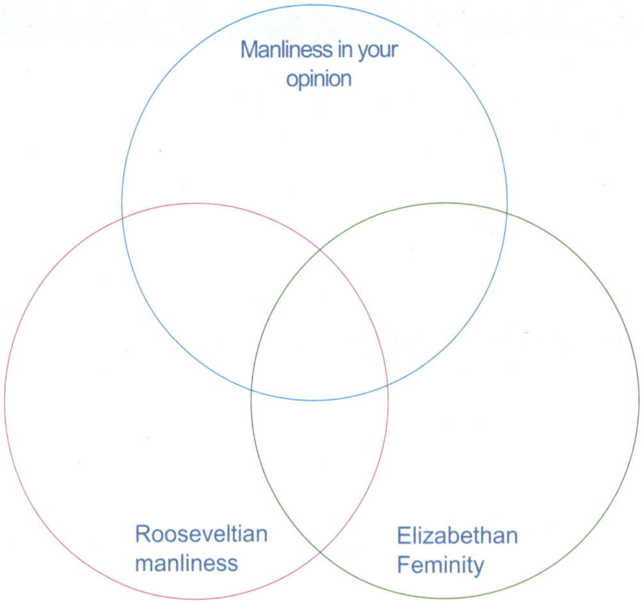

#3

Roosevelt was a Social Darwinist. How did his Social Darwinism differ from Cecil Rhodes?

#4

Korean manliness and popular behavior for young Korean men is different. Who is a good example of Korean manliness?

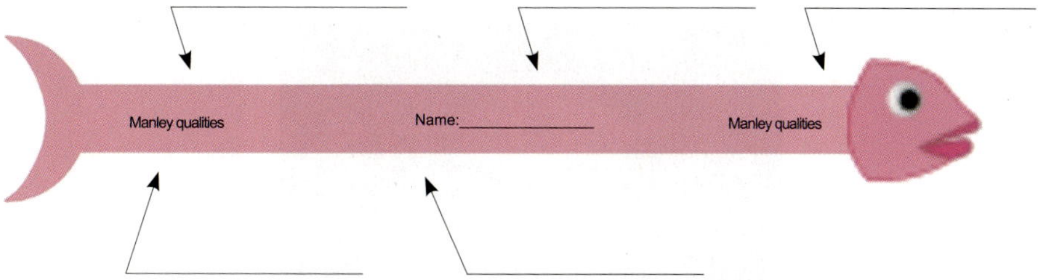

#5

Imagine womanly ideal Elizabeth met manly ideal Roosevelt. Do you think they would be friends?

11

Malcolm X and Black Nationalism

Malcolm X speaking shortly before his death.

Pre-reading vocabulary and phrases

black nationalism	strong pride in the black race
spread the word	make something widely known
marked for death	to be the target of assassination

흑인 민족주의는 1950년대, 60년대와 70년대의 미국의 흑인들 사이에 대중적이었던 믿음으로 흑인들이 백인들과 절대로 함께 생활할 수 없다는 내용을 포함하고 있습니다. "소프트(soft)" 흑인 민족주의는 미국에 거주하고 있는 흑인들이 미국을 떠나서 흑인들의 나라를 건설하자는 이념을 가지고 있습니다. "하드(hard)" 흑인 민족주의는 백인들은 유전적으로 열등하거나 필연적이게 악의를 가지고 있다는 이념을 바탕으로 하고 있습니다. 각각의 경우에, 흑인들이 백인들과 같이 공존하기를 시도하는 대신 흑인의 사회를 개선하는데 초점을 맞춰야 한다고 주장하고 있습니다.

There are certain neighborhoods in Philadelphia, Los Angeles and Detroit where white people should not go. Actually, Asian, Hispanic and Indian people should not go to these neighborhoods, either. In these neighborhoods, black people are sometimes hostile to people of other races.

These neighborhoods often have their own rules. The police sometimes don't come into these neighborhoods and strong, local citizens make the real laws. The morality in these neighborhoods comes from the communities. It is often different from the mainstream moral systems. It is often *intentionally different.**

These neighborhoods often have many Muslims and very hostile feelings toward white people. Sometimes they have a lot of crime, sometimes they have nearly no crime. These neighborhoods never, however, want to be part of mainstream, white American culture.*

African American boys attending a Nation of Islam speech in San Francisco

Where did this hostility come from? Why, even today, is there strain between white and black Americans? The obvious answer is slavery, but slavery ended 150 years ago. Unfortunately, the truth is that, in some ways, the relationship between white and black people actually became worse from the end of slavery until the 1960's. Even in modern times, many black people feel threatened by white culture and many white people feel threatened by black culture. The life of Malcolm X provides a good case study.*

Malcolm Little was born in 1925 in Nebraska. His mother Louise Little was a housewife and his father, Earl Little, was a minister who preached black nationalism. Because of Earl Little's black nationalism, a white racist organization threatened to kill the Little family several times. When Malcolm was 4 years old, the white racists burned the Little house to the ground. Two years later, they killed Earl Little by crushing his skull and throwing him onto the train tracks. This caused Louise Little to suffer a mental breakdown and, as such, she lost her children to foster homes and orphanages.

White Americans celebrating the murder of a black man in the 1930's. White Americans killed Malcolm's father in 1930, as well. Photo credit Leemage/Getty Images

Malcolm Little was a smart, focused student until middle school. He was the best student in his classes and wanted to be a lawyer. However, his favorite white teacher told him that being a lawyer "is not a realistic goal for a nigger." (Nigger is an extremely rude word for "black person.") This caused Malcolm Little to lose interest in school and drop out. By the time he had turned 17, Malcolm Little was selling drugs, controlling prostitutes and running illegal gambling activities.

Discussion Topic: Imagine that white people treated you like they treated Malcolm X. How would this change your life?

Police eventually caught him in 1946 and sent him to prison. Malcolm Littlehad to spend 7 years in prison for burglary. He used his time in prison to develop his education. He read the dictionary several times to improve his vocabulary.He also read about history, religion and philosophy and became involved with the Black Muslim movement.

The Black Muslims were officially called The Nation of Islam and followed Elijah Muhammad. Muhammad taught that white people were devils sent from hell to torment Blacks, Hispanics, Arabs and Asians. Where Martin Luther King wanted black and white people to live together as equals, Muhammad wanted blacks to leave America and start their own country. As Malcolm Little studied the work of Elijah Muhammad, he became more and more interested in the Nation of Islam. Malcolm Little, at that time, renounced his "slave name" of Little and started calling himself Malcolm X.

본 장에서 말하는 「The Nation of Islam」은 일반적인 「이슬람」종교와 큰 차이가 있습니다. The Nation of Islam은 백인들이 다른 인종들을 고문하기 위해 지옥에서 보내졌다고 가르치고 있습니다. 더 나아가 흑인들이 세상에서 가장 우수한 인종이라고 믿고 있습니다. 이에 반해 「이슬람」종교는 인종과 상관없이 누구나 이슬람교 신자가 될 수 있으며, 이슬람교 창시자로 알려진 무하메드는 어떠한 인종도 다른 인종에 비해 우수하거나 열등하다고 주장하지 않습니다.

Nation of Islam leader Elijah Muhammad.

Malcolm X's intelligence and speaking skill helped him to move up quickly within the Nation of Islam. He became the national spokesman and established many new mosques in Detroit and New York. He used newspapers, radio and television interviews to spread the word about the Nation of Islam. Because of Malcolm X's exceptional work, the membership of the Nation of Islam increased from about 500 members in 1952 to over 30,000 in 1963.

Malcolm X was hugely controversial and was in constant demand by the media. This was good for recruitment, but it set up the beginnings of a conflict between Malcolm X and Elijah Muhammad. This was because although Muhammad was the leader of the Nation of Islam, he was nowhere near as famous as Malcolm X, nor as talented. As such, Muhammad felt threatened by Malcolm. This caused Malcolm X a great deal of anxiety.

The big problems began in 1963 when Malcolm discovered that Elijah Muhammad had been having sex with his teenaged secretaries, a major sin in the Nation of Islam. Some of these affairs resulted in children. Muhammad asked Malcolm X to help cover up the affairs but Malcolm refused and, because of Muhammad' s hypocrisy, Malcolm X began to feel ashamed of leading so many people into the "fraudulent" Nation of Islam. In 1964, Malcolm X left the Nation of Islam and took a trip to Mecca.

Malcolm X visits Nigeria during his Hajj trip in 1964.

This was the first time Malcolm X could experience Islam outside the Nation of Islam and it changed his entire way of looking at life. He met blond haired, blue eyed Muslims "I could call my brothers." He saw different cultures mixing and living together peacefully for the first time. It was also the first time he'd given an interview to support anybody who wasn't black.

This caused even more tension with the Nation of Islam and, in late 1964, Elijah Muhammad's organization marked Malcolm X for death. Undercover FBI agents in the Nation of Islam reported several assassination attempts, including fire bombing and car bombings. Finally, in February of 1965, three Nation of Islam assassins shot Malcolm X 15 times while he spoke, killing him. He was 39 years old.

Malcolm defends his family from Nation of Islam assassins.

Speech 2: Return from Mecca

Reporter 1: Malcolm, on your trip abroad you said you sensed a feeling of great brotherhood and conceivably might be working toward integration in this country now. At least this is what you're reported to have said. Any comment on that?

Malcolm X: I don't think I ever mentioned anything about working towards integration. If I recall, I pointed out that while I was at Mecca making the pilgrimage I spoke about the brotherhood that existed at all levels and among all people who were there on that Hajj, who had accepted the religion of Islam. And I pointed out what the religion of Islam had done over there for those people, who despite their complexion differences, that it would probably do America well to study the religion of Islam. Perhaps it could drive some of the racism from this society as it has driven racism from the Muslim society.

Reporter 2: Isn't the integration drive aiming for this goal?

Malcolm X: I can't say the integration drive is aiming for this goal because it hasn't realized the goal in any state. They haven't even gotten integration here in New York City. You have worse integration problems in the North than they have in the South. So if you can't bring about integration in New York City, as international, cosmopolitan and up to date as it's supposed to be, you will never get integration anywhere else in the country.

Reporter 3: Malcolm, have your experiences with white skinned Muslims in Africa and the Middle East made you feel that relations between negroes and whites who are not Muslims is any more possible?

Malcolm X: When I was on the pilgrimage I had close contact with Muslims whose skin would, in America, be classified as white and with Muslims who would themselves be classified as white in America. But these particular Muslims didn't call themselves white. They looked upon themselves as human beings, as part of the human family and therefore they looked upon all other segments of the human family as part of the same family. They had a different look or a different air or a different attitude than that which is reflected in the attitude of the man in America who calls himself white. So I said that if Islam had done this for them, perhaps if the white man in America would study Islam, perhaps it would do the same thing for him.

Reporter 4: I think what a lot of people are interested in, Malcolm, is whether this experience has made your feelings change, that the animosity you have expressed in the past to all whites –

Malcolm X: There's one thing I want to make quite clear. No matter how much respect, no matter how much recognition whites show towards me, as far as I'm concerned, as long as that same respect is not shown to every one of our people in this country, it doesn't exist for me. (Applause)

Reporter 5: Are you prepared to go to the United Nations and demand that charges be brought against the United States for its treatment of negroes?

Malcolm X: Oh yes. As I pointed out, when I was on my trip, that African nations and Asian nations and Latin American nations look very hypocritical when they stand up in the United Nations condemning the racist practices of South Africa and that which is practiced by Portugal and Angola and say nothing in the UN about the racist practices that are manifest everyday against negroes in this society. Even in South Africa, those Africans aren't faced with bayonets and aren't faced with police dogs. When I was in Beirut, I saw a picture on the front page of a negro being beaten in Tennessee. When I got to Cairo, I saw the same picture of a negro being beaten in Tennessee. When I got to Lagos, I saw the same picture.

So with these African nations knowing the brutality that is being inflicted on black people in this country simply because those black people are trying to get what the Supreme Court said they should get 10 years ago. I would not be a man if I were in a position to bring this to the United Nations and did not do so.

Reporter 6: Have you had any commitment from any of the nations in Africa?

Malcolm X: The one thing I found in my travels is that all of the Africans but also the Asians and Muslims look upon us as their long-lost brothers and America had actually tricked many of them into a hands off policy by giving the impression that she was honestly trying to do something to solve the problem. My argument over there was designed to prove that it is impossible for the United States government to solve the race problem. It is impossible for a government which has 16 senatorial committees over which 10 are chaired by southern segregationists and 20 congressional committees, over which a Southern segregationist chairs. This is a segregationist, racist government that's controlled by people from the South. They can't solve the race problem.

Reporter 1: Do you plan to take part in the political campaign this fall?

Malcolm X: I intend to take part in anything that will get results, that eliminates the injustices our people are confronted with in this country, politically, economically, anything.

Reporter 1: Do you intend to work with the leaders of some of the other civil rights organizations?

Malcolm X: Certainly. We will work with any groups, organizations or leaders in any way as long as it's genuinely designed to get results.

Resources	
For more information on race relations in America, visit http://www.brookings.edu/research/articles/1998/03/spring-poverty-loury	
For more information on black nationalism and separatism, see "The Autobiography of Malcolm X." http://book.naver.com/bookdb/book_detail.nhn?bid=3426464	
For more information about how blacks are perceived in the West, visit https://www.psychologytoday.com/blog/culturally-speaking/201112/african-americans-and-pathological-stereotypes	
https://www.psychologytoday.com/blog/culturally-speaking/201112/the-circular-nature-pathological-stereotypes	

#1

Imagine you grew up like Malcolm X did? How would you think about white people?

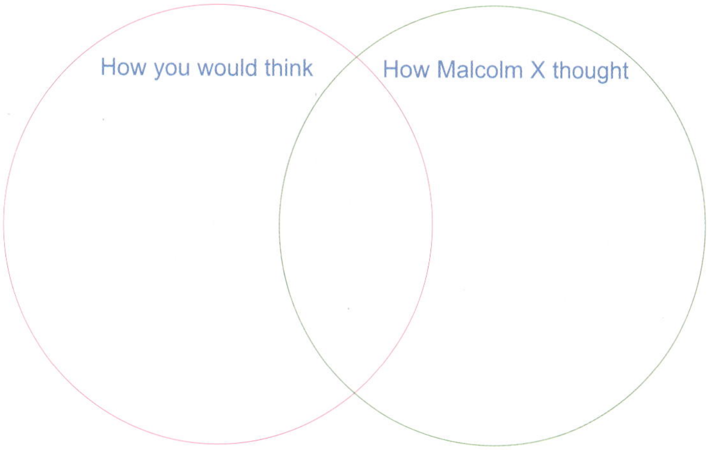

#2

Cecil Rhodes and Malcolm X believed very strongly in racial differences. How were they similar and different?

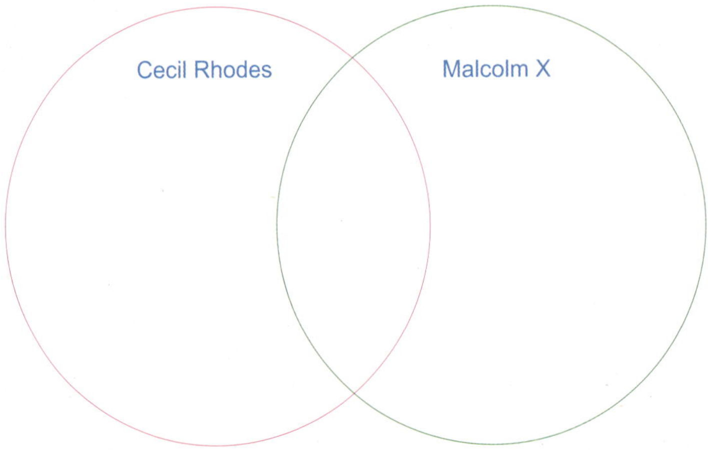

#3

How are Kim Gu's feelings about the Japanese similar or different from Malcolm X's feelings about white people?

Kim Gu on the Japanese	Malcolm X on white people
1.	1.
2.	2.
3.	3.

#4

(Survey) Ask at least 3 students what is more important, culture or race? Discuss your findings.

#5

I think Malcolm X was better before/after Mecca because ....

12

Anti-Communism and the Modern American Conservative

Senator Joseph McCarthy

Pre-reading vocabulary and phrases

Marshall Plan	a policy created by the United States to rebuild countries destroyed during World War Two
welfare program	money or help that a government gives to people who are poor or do not have jobs
witch hunt	an attempt to find and punish people whose opinions are unpopular
arms race	a contest between two or more countries to build up the most powerful possible militaries
when the chips are down	when a situation is very serious
State Department	the part of the US government that deals with foreign matters
American exceptionalism	the belief that the United States is unique and cannot be judged the same ways other countries are judged

Advertisement from 1950 encourages Americans to fight against "communist controlled" radio and television programs in America. Advertisement from the 1960's warns Americans that communists want black men to marry white women and ruin the white race. Advertisement from 2010 says President Obama's healthcare program is secretly communist.

According to the William Jefferson Clinton Memorial Library, a group dedicated to stopping socialism and communism, President Bill Clinton was a socialist. Clinton wanted to control all businesses and tell everyone what they could and couldn't buy. His real goal, the William Jefferson Clinton Memorial Library says, was to "introduce the Socialist State that Barack Obama later codified in America." This included an evil plan to control all people's salaries, help the government take away people's ability to choose doctors and to criminalize all free economic choices.*

The William Jefferson Clinton Memorial Library goes on to explain that, in Bill Clinton or Barack Obama's desired society, citizens will become the property of the central government. This way, Bill Clinton and Barack Obama can control all American people's decisions about education, hobbies and even the ways to raise children.

While the Clinton Memorial Library is relatively extreme in its views, there are a large number of Americans who basically agree with these ideas. 55% of Americans, at one time, believed that Barack Obama was a socialist, for example.* This seems very strange to most Koreans, who view the United States as a super-capitalist country. Why, then, is there such a difference in perception? In order to answer this question, we need to learn about the history of anti-communism in the United States.

The United States has two main political parties. The American Democrats are roughly similar to the Democratic Party (새정치민주연합) in South Korea. Perhaps a little bit more conservative on economic issues, a little bit more liberal on social issues, but roughly similar. The other major American party, the conservative Republican Party, is unlike anything in Korea or, indeed, most of the rest of the world. American conservatives, while strange to most Koreans, are very common and powerful. They are approximately 35% of the population and they' ve won 6 of the last 10 presidential elections. To help you understand what Republicans believe and why they believe it, we should start with the immediate aftermath of World War II.

In the few years after 1945, Americans were feeling very confident. They had been largely responsible for defeating Nazism, the Japanese Imperialists and they had unlocked the power of nuclear weapons. Further, the American Marshal Plan* was rebuilding Western Europe into the peaceful, rich place it is today and a similarly successful program was unfolding in Japan. There did not seem to be any credible threat to American power, there did not seem to be anything to stop a long period of Pax Americana. That is Latin for "American Peace" and it means global peace under American domination. There have also been periods called Pax Romana and Pax Britanica. In Asian history, there have been similar periods of peace under the Tang and Han Dynasties in China.

It was thus a huge shock when, in 1948, the Soviet Union exploded their first nuclear bomb. That the Soviet Union had used a network of spies to steal nuclear technology from US scientists made this even more unsettling.

Americans were right to fear the Soviet Union. Soviet leader Joseph Stalin had already killed tens of millions of people in his purges, and he was aggressively expanding communist controlled territory. China, as well, fell to Mao Zedong' s communist forces and soon the Chinese and North Koreans were threatening to take over all of the Korean Peninsula. China and the Soviet Union both supported efforts to destroy democracies. Suddenly, Europe and Asia, both of which had seemed safe, were in danger of communist takeovers.

지난 100년간 2명의 가장 파괴적인 지도자들이 모두 공산주의 국가에서 존재했었습니다. 마오쩌둥은 많게는 7천 5만 명 적어도 3천만 명을 학살했습니다. 요세프 스탈린은 2천만 명 정도를 학살했습니다. 이러한 이유로 인해 미국인들이 공산주의를 더욱 두려워하게 되었습니다.

This led to a backlash against a great many things in America. Conservative Americans began to see it as their duty to stop anything that even looked like a socialist or communist idea. Because communists want government to take care of poor people, American conservatives began to believe that programs to help the poor were secretly communist conspiracies. Because communists supported civil rights in America, many conservatives turned against civil rights. Because communists believe in large government, conservatives began to believe that all or most government was evil. This led to a revival of states' rights thinking, similar to the debate that caused the American Civil War. It also led to some unusual economic ideas that we will discuss in the next chapter.

One of the earliest, and certainly most famous of these anti-communist crusaders was Senator Joseph McCarthy. McCarthy expanded the fight against communists to attack lots of people, not just those helping the Soviet Union. He attacked artists who didn't like capitalism and movie directors who were insufficiently patriotic. Minority rights groups also became targets. He thought that since minority groups were challenging white American leadership, they must be helping the Soviet Union. He accused groups that wanted the government to help the poor of being secret communists, as well as leading a charge to punish the children of people who were connected to socialist or communist groups.

While McCarthy's "witch hunt" quickly reached the point of ridiculousness, it is important to remember that the anti-communist movement was based on real things. We now know that Soviet agents had indeed infiltrated the US government during and after WWII. We also know that Julius and Ethel Rosenberg, spies convicted in 1951, had indeed stolen nuclear secrets and given them to Stalin.

Addresses to the American People

Senator Joseph McCarthy

청색으로 쓰여진 문서는 원본 스크립트입니다. 반드시 읽어 보시길 권합니다. 진한 부분은 저자의 해설입니다. 원본을 단순화한 버전이 아닙니다.

Wheeling, West Virginia,

February 9, 1950

Five years after a world war has been won (in 1950), men's hearts should anticipate a long peace—and men's minds should be free from the heavy weight that comes with war. But this is not such a period—for this is not a period of peace. This is a time of "the cold war." This is a time when all the world is split into two vast, increasingly hostile armed camps—a time of a great armament race.

McCarthy is talking about the beginnings of the Cold War, an arms race between the US and the Soviet Union.

Today we can almost physically hear the mutterings and rumblings of an invigorated god of war. You can see it, feel it, and hear it all the way from the Indochina hills, from the shores of Formosa, right over into the very heart of Europe itself.

McCarthy believed that the Cold War would get worse and threaten the safety of the entire world. He was correct.

"The Indo-China hills" refers to the communist takeover of China in 1949. Formosa is an old name for Taiwan. McCarthy is also referring to the communist takeover of East Germany, Hungary and much of Eastern Europe happening in the late 1940s.

The one encouraging thing is that the "mad moment" has not yet arrived for the firing of the gun or the exploding of the bomb which will set civilization about the final task of destroying itself. There is still a hope for peace if we finally decide that no longer can we safely blind our eyes and close our ears to those facts which are shaping up more and more clearly, and that is that we are now engaged in a show-down fight, not the usual war between nations for land areas or other material gains, but a war between two diametrically opposed ideologies.

The "mad moment" is using a nuclear weapon. McCarthy believes Americans must have an ideological fight against all communists everywhere, not just those in the Soviet Union or communist China.

The great difference between our western Christian world and the atheistic Communist world is not political, gentlemen, it is moral. For instance, the Marxian idea of confiscating the land and factories and running the entire economy as a single enterprise is momentous. Likewise, Lenin's invention of the one-party police state as a way to make Marx's idea work is hardly less momentous.

McCarthy, here, says that communism is a moral evil, not a political evil.

Stalin's resolute putting across of these two ideas, of course, did much to divide the world. With only these differences, however, the east and the west could most certainly still live in peace.

The real, basic difference, however, lies in the religion of immoralism – invented by Marx, preached feverishly by Lenin, and carried to unimaginable extremes by Stalin. This religion of immoralism, if the Red half of the world triumphs—and well it may, gentlemen—this religion of immoralism will more deeply wound and damage mankind than any conceivable economic or political system.

This is a gross misrepresentation of the truth. Marx considered his ideology a MORE moral system than capitalism or democracy. So did Lenin and Mao and the vast majority of communists throughout history. Human beings are very good at morally justifying horrible things and bad intentions are not necessary to destroy lots and lots of lives.

Karl Marx dismissed God as a hoax, and Lenin and Stalin have added in clear-cut, unmistakable language their resolve that no nation, no people who believe in a god, can exist side by side with their communistic state.

This is technically true, although communists have tolerated and continue to tolerate limited amounts of religious belief in the people.

Karl Marx, for example, expelled people from his Communist Party for mentioning such things as love, justice, humanity or morality. He called this "soulful ravings" and "sloppy sentimentality."

This is an enormous distortion of the truth. Karl Marx did not oppose love, justice, humanity or morality. McCarthy is either ignorant or lying here.

Today we are engaged in a final, all-out battle between communistic atheism and Christianity. The modern champions of communism have selected this as the time, and ladies and gentlemen, the chips are down—they are truly down.

McCarthy believes that when the chips are down, we must stand up to communists.

Lest there be any doubt that the time has been chosen, let us go directly to the leader of communism today—Joseph Stalin. Here is what he said—not back in 1928, not before the war, not during the war—but 2 years after the last war was ended: "To think that the Communist revolution can be carried out peacefully, within the framework of a Christian democracy, means one has either gone out of one's mind and lost all normal understanding, or has grossly and openly repudiated the Communist revolution."

Most communists did believe that making a country communist required an armed struggle. In other words, McCarthy is right about this.

Ladies and gentlemen, can there be anyone tonight who is so blind as to say that the war is not on? Can there by anyone who fails to realize that the Communist world has said the time is now? That this is the time for the show-down between the democratic Christian world and the communistic atheistic world?

Unless we face this fact, we shall pay the price that must be paid by those who wait too long.

Basically, if Americans wait too long, they are going to be killed.

Six years ago, there was within the Soviet orbit, 180,000,000 people. Lined up on the anti-totalitarian side there were in the world at that time, roughly 1,625,000,000 people.

Today, only six years later, there are 800,000,000 people under the absolute domination of Soviet Russia—an increase of over 400 percent. On our side, the figure has shrunk to around 500,000,000. In other words, in less than six years, the odds have changed from 9 to 1 in our favor to 8 to 5 against us.

This is not really true. The Soviet Union had 180,000,000 people in 1950. China had about 550,000,000. There were very few other communist countries of any size at the time in a world population of 2,600,000,0000 people.

This indicates the swiftness of the tempo of Communist victories and American defeats in the Cold War. As one of our outstanding historical figures once said, "When a great democracy is destroyed, it will not be from enemies from without, but rather because of enemies from within."

The reason why we find ourselves in a position of impotency is not because our only powerful potential enemy has sent men to invade our shores, but rather because of the traitorous actions of those who have been treated so well by this Nation. It has not been the less fortunate, or members of minority groups who have been traitorous to this Nation, but rather those who have had all the benefits that the wealthiest Nation on earth has had to offer, the finest homes, the finest college education and the finest jobs in government we can give.

McCarthy claims that American traitors are the reason communists have won in Eastern Europe and China.

This is glaringly true in the State Department. There the bright young men who are born with silver spoons in their mouths are the ones who have been most traitorous. . . .

The State Department (국무부) is full of communist traitors, McCarthy says.

I have here in my hand a list of 205 . . . a list of names that were made known to the Secretary of State as being members of the Communist Party and who nevertheless are still working and shaping policy in the State Department. . . .

McCarthy was probably lying about the list of communists. Most historians think the list never existed.* However, newly released Soviet documents show there were secret communists in the government. McCarthy, though, was never able to show any evidence for his accusations.

As you know, very recently the Secretary of State proclaimed his loyalty to a man guilty of what has always been considered as the most abominable of all crimes—being a traitor to the people who gave him a position of great trust—high treason. . . .

McCarthy is referring to Alger Hiss. Hiss may have been a spy, but that remains controversial.

He has lighted the spark which is resulting in a moral uprising and will end only when the whole sorry mess of twisted, warped thinkers are swept from the national scene so that we may have a new birth of honesty and decency in government.

McCarthy's Victims

While it is important to remember how frightening communism in the 1950's was, (Josef Stalin and Mao Zedong are numbers one and two on the list of history's greatest mass murderers) we should also not forget the consequences of the McCarthy witch hunt. Dozens of innocent people were taken before the House Un-American Activities Committee and unfairly punished. McCarthy and his allies also "blacklisted" dozens of artists throughout the Western World.

According to Martin E. Eigenberger's study in "Psychological Reports," there is a strong correlation between the level of fear people experience and how likely they are to support authoritarianism. McCarthy understood this and used fear of communism to support his authoritarian attacks on liberals, intellectuals and artists in general.

McCarthy personally attacked and damaged the careers of celebrities like the famous direction Orson Welles, comedian and actor Charlie Chaplin and poet Langston Hughes. However, far more important, McCarthy used the fear of communism to punish thought.

McCarthy repeatedly investigated the economist Val Lorwin for treason not because he had evidence, but simply because Lorwin supported Scandanavian style socialism, which McCarthy disliked. In fact, Lorwin had been an anti-communist for several years before McCarthy rose to power. None of these facts mattered, though, as McCarthy's attacks resulted in Lorwin being fired and charged with crimes several times, though he was never convicted. McCarthy also attempted to destroy East Asia expert Owen Lattimore. This case was even more ridiculous than the attacks on Lorwin. McCarthy accused Lattimore of being a spy based on two pieces of evidence. First, McCarthy believed that American spies must have been responsible for China becoming communist in 1949. Lattimore had lived and studied in China and therefore seemed "suspicious." The second piece of evidence were witnesses who maybe, possibly could remember a time when Lattimore might have said something sympathetic to Josef Stalin or "smiled at a strange time." When these attacks failed, McCarthy and his allies tried to convict Lattimore of "not being active enough in the fight against communism." Judges later cleared Lattimore of all charges.

Investigations later showed that FBI agents and prosecutors had been so afraid of making McCarthy angry that they'd indicted people on poor evidence rather than risk becoming McCarthy's next victim.

Resources	
For more information on the William Jefferson Clinton Memorial Library and their communist fears, visit http://www.clintonmemoriallibrary.com/socialist_agenda.html	
For more information on Americans' perceptions on socialism, visit http://www.theatlantic.com/business/archive/2010/07/poll-55-of-likely-voters-think-obama-is-a-socialist/59463/	
For more information about the Marshall Plan, visit http://elevenbuilding.tistory.com/536	
For more information on McCarthy's lists, visit http://www.washington.edu/news/2014/10/14/documents-that-changed-the-world-joseph-mccarthys-list-1950/	

#1

Compare American and Korean anti-communism.

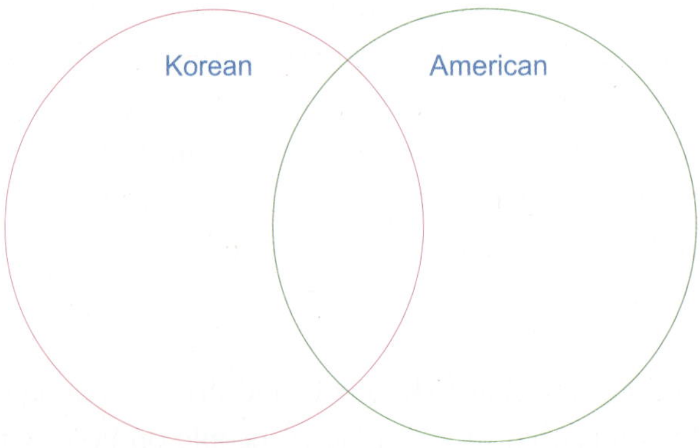

#2

Do you think McCarthy's with-hunts are similar to Chun Doo-Hwan's 5.18.1981 Gwanju Massacre? Why or why not?

#3

Is American anti-communism a self-contained philosophy or is it just a reaction to communism?

Real philosophy	Just a reaction	Something else
1.	1.	1.
2.	2.	2.

#4

What do you think Theodore Roosevelt would say about McCarthy?

#5

Why did conservatives learn to distrust almost all government?

Spies	
McCarthy	
Other	

#6

Is it possible to be anti-communist if you AREN'T afraid? Take a survey of classmates' answers. Present at least two different opinions?

#7

Should it be illegal to believe in communism? List 3 reasons for "yes" and three reasons for "no".

Yes (illegal)	1.
	2.
	3.
No (legal)	1.
	2.
	3.

13

Libertarianism and the Reagan Revolution

Former US president Ronald Reagan

Pre-reading vocabulary and phrases

The Great Leap Forward	a Chinese communist plan to develop the economy from 1958 to 1962 that killed at least 18,000,000 people
The Cultural Revolution	a Chinese communist plan to make China more communist and more pure that lasted from 1966 to 1976 and killed between 750,000 and 10,000,000 people
hawks and doves	supporters of aggressive military action and supporters of pacifism, respectively
burden of proof	the responsibility for proving something
altruism	willingness to do things that bring advantages to others, even if it results in disadvantage for yourself
welfare recipient	a person who receives money or assistance from the government
collectivism	a theory or political system based on the principle that all of the farms, factories and other places of work in a country should be owned by or for all the people in that country

The anti-communist forces in the US and England became stronger throughout the 1970s and 1980s, probably peaking in the mid 80s. The huge numbers of deaths caused by the Chinese Communist Party and the Soviet Union made Americans and Englishmen even more afraid of communism than they had been. Examples of communist outrages include the Great Leap Forward and Cultural Revolution in China, where an estimated 30,000,000 people died. The Soviet Union committed similar atrocities in Hungary, Poland and Afghanistan.

Americans and British people, understandably, wanted to be nothing like the communist countries. This manifested in the beliefs of people like US President Ronald Reagan and British Prime Minister Margaret Thatcher. Communists wanted to take all of a person's money and use it in the government, so anti-communists wanted to take as little as possible. Communists wanted to have the government control industries, so anti-communists wanted the industries to be free from government influence. Communists wanted a powerful, central government, so anti-communists wanted a small government with states' rights.

US President and Libertarian hero Ronald Reagan meeting friend and fellow Libertarian hero, UK Prime Minister Margaret Thatcher.

Ronald Reagan was the first person to make the economic portion of anti-communism into government policy. He weakened labor unions, lowered taxes on rich people, got rid of many environmental controls and lessened the regulation of many industries. He also united religions conservatives, libertarians and anti-communist hawks into the Reagan coalition that dominated US politics from 1980 all the way until 2006.

Reagan, with his belief that individual Americans could overcome interference from the government and become successful, inspired millions of Americans. This was a huge shift from the left wing government of previous President, Jimmy Carter. Where Carter and the liberals had encouraged Americans to think of their mistakes and sins, Reagan told Americans to believe in their own fundamental goodness. Where Carter's presidency had been consumed with feelings of weakness, Reagan projected an image of America that was strong, glorious and a model for the rest of the world's countries. It is difficult to overstate how big an impact this shift had on American culture.

The United Kingdom had a similar experience with Margaret Thatcher. The "Iron Lady" thought that the United Kingdom had been overtaken by weak, self-hating socialists. Emphasizing hard work, self-reliance and toughness, Thatcher was able to crush labor unions, deregulate business and grow the British economy. Life certainly became worse for the poor, but Thatcher's UK, like Reagan's US, saw a big shift towards individualism, hope and admiration for the wealthy.

Both Thatcher and Reagan are remembered as great leaders in their countries. Reagan is the most popular American president since John Kennedy and Thatcher is the most popular prime minister since WW2.

Please watch this video on the Reagan Revolution:

http://www.youtube.com/watch?v=2h4DkpFP_aw

Libertarianism

Senator Barry Goldwater helped make Libertarianism popular in America

While Libertarianism is inspired by philosophers and economists like John Locke, David Hume, Thomas Jefferson, Thomas Paine and Adam Smith, it is much different from those early, liberal thinkers. Libertarianism did not become popular until the early 1960s with the rise of Senator Barry Goldwater and author Ayn Rand. Ever since, Libertarianism has been a major force in US politics, much more so than any other major nation. Let's look at what Libertarians believe.

Individualism: Individualism in English has a different connotation than the Korean word for individualism(개인주의). When a Korean person thinks of individualism he or she will imagine selfishness, greed and immaturity. When an American or British person says individualism, they think of someone who is brave, independent and strong. Libertarians believe that the individual person's freedom is more important than the cohesion of the group. They think individual choice is the most important thing in life. Libertarians try to defend the right to make individual choices. They want everyone to be responsible for their individual choices.

Individual Rights: Libertarians believe that the right to life, liberty and property is natural. They believe that the government does not give these rights, but that nature gives these rights inherently. People who want to take away freedoms have the burden of proof.

Natural Social Structures: Libertarians believe that most human social structures arise naturally. Thousands or millions of people, just by behaving normally, create stable social institutions. Libertarians believe that language, law, money, economics and social norms all developed without a government plan, and as such, we almost never need the government to make social structures. Instead of government plans, we should let individual people make their own social organizations. When people try to make plans for society, they will almost always fail. When they let society be natural and uncontrolled, it will work better.

Naturally Convergent Interests: Libertarians believe that people in a good society naturally have the same interests (goals). In a just, free society, factory owners will naturally oppose polluting the water just as much as fishermen oppose polluting water. Oil companies will naturally oppose CO2 pollution and farmers will naturally want to stop cutting down trees for more farmland. It is only when the government uses force that naturally harmonious businesses come into conflict with each other and the general public. Anyone who is not naturally harmonious is probably a criminal.

Discussion Topic: What are some naturally convergent interests you have with parents, friends or your bosses?

Lawfulness: Libertarians believe that no individual can act in a way that takes away someone else's freedom. Libertarians want to follow laws, but they only like laws that individuals make. If the government makes the laws, that's bad. No politicians should design the laws. Instead, the laws should be naturally made by lawsuits. If we have more lawsuits, Libertarians believe, we can also get rid of government regulatory agencies. This way, the government cannot control people but people who need regulatory protection can sue offenders. Libertarians want to enforce these unplanned laws very strictly.

Small Government: Libertarians believe you need a government to protect rights and enforce laws, but that government is always dangerous. Any group that is powerful, like a government can be, should be treated with suspicion. As such, Libertarians want the government to be weak and small, so that it cannot oppress people. Making the government small is extremely important to Libertarians. If the government is small, Libertarians believe, freedom and economic growth will follow.

Lassez Faire*(pronounced leɪ.seɪ ˌfeə(ɹ))*: People need to buy and sell if they want to be successful. People have a natural right to property and a natural right to exchange that property with others. In order to use these rights, people need capitalist markets and everything will be better if the government doesn't interfere. Free economics is better than regulated economics.

Keeping What You Earn: Libertarians believe you should be able to keep the things you earn. They oppose transferring money or things from people who produce wealth to those who have the power to take that wealth. For example, it is wrong to take tax money from a wealthy businessman and give it to a beggar. In other words, Libertarians oppose taxation, especially when the tax money goes to government employees or welfare recipients.

Ayn Rand, Believing in the Power of Heroes

Philosopher and writer Ayn Rand is one of the most controversial figures in American history and a huge influence on both Libertarians and American conservatives generally. Born into a wealthy, Jewish family in Russia, Rand's elementary and middle school years were spent in comfort and privilege. She was friends with the famous Nabakov literary family, lived in luxurious homes and had access to the finest education. However, the communist Russian Revolution took place during Rand's early teens and almost destroyed her life.

The Russian communists, advocating for equality and fairness, murdered millions of Russian intellectuals, business people and aristocrats. Rand watched first hand as the altruistic communists crushed freedom of speech, free thought and de-emphasized the importance of individual people in favor of the collective. Communists stole her hard-working father's business and forced the family out of their home. During this time, the family occasionally starved, but Rand was able to start her college education (Russian women had not been allowed to study in college before the communists took over). However, shortly before graduating, communist officials purged Rand for coming from a business-owning family. Rand was able to get a visa to visit family in the United States in 1926. She would never return to Russia.

In the US, Rand discovered capitalism, individualism and the heroic nature of greed. Remembering the horrible things altruistic communists had done to her family and native country, Rand devoted her life to defeating collectivism, altruism and economic redistribution. She created a new system of morality, called "Objectivism," based on the idea that the highest good any person could achieve was following his or her own rational self-interest.

She started her career by working part time jobs in Hollywood, eventually married an actor and grew into a successful novelist and philosopher. With her trademark long cigarettes and intense personality, Rand became one of the biggest celebrities in the US. In her two most famous books, Atlas Shrugged and The Fountainhead, the heroes are self-made individualists who overcome constant attacks from sickly, corrupt altruists. In Atlas Shrugged, all the wonderful business men and women of the world join with scientists and artists to make an individualist paradise. By leaving for the paradise all at once, the virtuous individualists doom evil government officials, communists and poor people to chaos and destruction. In the Fountainhead, heroic architect Howard Roark sacrifices his greatest artistic works rather than allow the government to control his individuality.

Rand died in 1982, but her books still sell millions of copies. Influential American politicians like former President George Bush and former Central Bank leader Alan Greenspan, business leaders like Steve Jobs and celebrities like Brad Pitt have all cited Rand as an inspiration for their work.

#1

Choose one of the following people and explain their ideas to your classmates: Milton Friedman, Friedrich Hayek, Ron Paul, Barry Goldwater, William Goodwin, Henry David Thoreau, H.L Mencken, Albert Jay Nock, Isabel Paterson, Rose Wilder Lane or Leonard E. Read.

#2

How successful was the Reagan Revolution?

Successes	Failures
1.	1.
2.	2.

#3

Why do you think Americans liked Reagan so much?

#4

Analyze libertarianism.

Good ideas	Bad ideas	Not sure
1.	1.	1.
2.	2.	2.
3	3	3

#5

Are there naturally convergent interests in business? Find at least 1 pro and 1 con example.

#6

Choose 1 Libertarian ideal and explain how it would work in Korea. Ideal ________________.

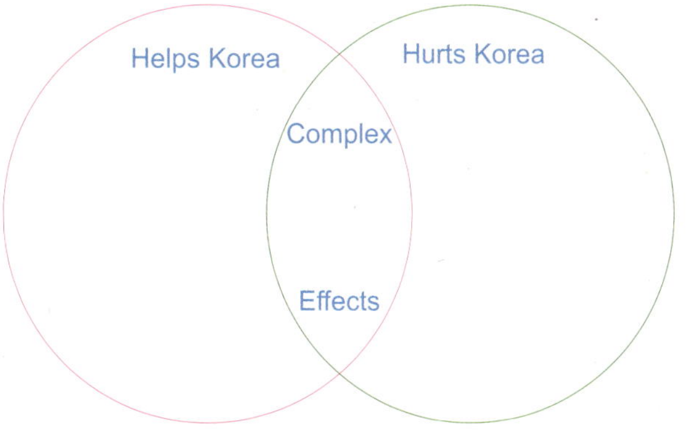

14

How a Burrito can Explain the Melting Pot

Burrito with rice, chicken, cheese, avocado, lettuce, tomatoes and a flour tortilla.

Pre-reading vocabulary and phrases

cater	to provide food
hunter-gatherer	a person who lives by hunting wild animals and gathering wild plants
domesticate	to bring animals or plants under human control in order to provide food, power or companionship
round up	gather together
rip off	to make a fake or illegal copy of something
emblematic	representing a particular person, group or idea

The burrito is one of the most popular foods in the English speaking world. There are dozens of styles of burrito including beef, chicken, pork and vegetarian varieties. Some burritos are easily eaten with your hands. Some are covered with green chili sauce while others are prepared with melted cheese and tomato salsa. The one, consistent characteristic of any burrito is that it will be wrapped in a tortilla.

Convenience store burrito, frozen burritos in a grocery store, hand-making a burrito

You can get a burrito in a huge number of restaurants. You can buy frozen burritos in grocery stores or microwaveable burritos at most convenience stores. Most Americans and a good percentage of English people can make a burrito at home. In Texas, you can visit burrito festivals with live country music. In the United Kingdom, you can ask a company called "Go Burrito" to cater for your wedding. If you want something that's emblematic of the English speaking world, the burrito is a pretty good choice, which is more than a little bit ironic.

That's because the burrito is a really, really inauthentic emblem. Even the word is foreign to English-speakers – burrito means "little donkey" in Spanish. The beans, far from originating in the US, were first cultivated by a pre-historic Peruvian culture around 9,000 years ago. No English farmer with a tractor, but men and women of some lost tribe of hunter-gathers just learning the secrets of agriculture.

The great city of Tenochtitlan, one of the earliest places to use tortillas

Meso-American Indians, the ancestors to the Aztecs and Mayans, invented the tortilla, made the first guacamole and domesticated the first chili peppers. You can imagine Aztecs working in floating gardens eating burritos.

The creamy cheese melting on top of the burrito above comes from at least 5,500 years ago in Sumer, and probably much earlier. If you are imagining the English Tesco foods corporation when you think of cheese's origins, the truth is that ancient and not at all English figures like Hector and Achilles would have enjoyed cheese snacks during lulls in the Trojan war.

Likewise the rice comes from the"authentically, all-American" farms of ancient China. If your burrito has pork, it is possible only because ancient people in Iraq domesticated wild boars. If your burrito has beef, then you really should thank the pre-historic Turks. If you prefer chicken, then you owe a debt to the people of India, circa 4,000 B.C.

So the ingredients of a burrito, a food popular in the English speaking world, are Peruvian/Mayan/Sumerian/Chinese/Turkish/Indian. The idea to combine these ingredients, at least, must be authentically Anglo-American, right? Not so, since the idea to combine rice, cheese, beans and meat in a tortilla most likely comes from a group of mixed race, Spanish-American Indian-African cowboys called "vaqueros."

South American vaquero rounding up cattle

This problem of finding authenticity in the English speaking world is not confined to burritos. The all-American pickup truck is the descendent of a French three wheeled cart. The definitively English "cup of tea" was blatantly ripped off of the Chinese. Hollywood is just an evolution of theaters in London and the theaters of London are recognizably the offspring of Roman and Greek theater. Rock and roll comes from the blues, which comes from a mixture of very old European church music and African folk music. Soccer (or football if you prefer) originated in England, but only if you forget that the Chinese and Greeks were playing almost exactly the same game thousands of years earlier. The authors of this book aren't sure what an authentically American or English thing would even look like.

And you can't escape this problem by talking about the Native Americans. If you look at the picture above, you will see an American Indian riding a Spanish horse using Portuguese horse riding techniques and holding a French-style gun. There is almost nothing authentic, just different ways of mixing bits of culture imported from somewhere else.

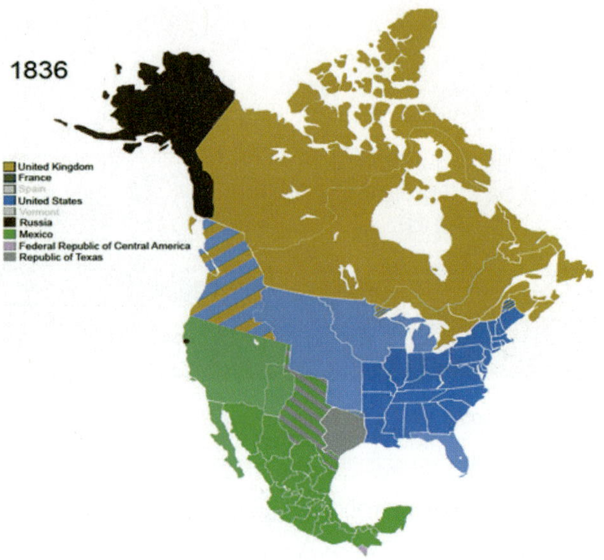

In 1800, land that is now part of the United States was controlled by France, Russia, Spain, Mexico, the Republic of Texas and Great Britain. The US has been a melting pot for its entire history.

This poses an interesting question for students in Korea, people like you. How much do you value authenticity? Melting pot societies like the United States and United Kingdom offer variety, they offer almost unlimited potential to mix and match new combinations but they make it hard to develop a distinctive culture. The United States doesn't really have anything distinctively American in the way that Koreans can claim Hangeul or kimchi.

Korea is becoming more and more open. Young people like you are going to need to decide how much authenticity your country maintains.

#1

How important is authenticity to you and your classmates? Discuss with at least two other students.

#2

How successful is the mixing of cultures in the UK and US?

Successes	Failures
1.	1.
2.	2.

#3

Why do you think it's hard to find authenticity in melting pot societies?

#4

Is there real authenticity in Korea? Find at least one reason there is authenticity and one reason there is not.

15

Fun Cultural Activities for Koreans Visiting the US, Canada or Great Britain.

Yoon-mi Jung, a contributor to this book, visiting an American family on vacation. Many foreign tourists stay with American families on vacation.

One of the best parts about traveling overseas is getting to try local sports, activities and customs. When Ben first came to Korea, for example, he was surprised and delighted to learn about traditional street markets, which he had never seen in the USA, badminton, which he had never played, and Korean poetry, which was really different from the poems he knew in the USA. The first time he went to a professional sports game in Korea, he was surprised and delighted to see how Koreans celebrate so openly – songs, cheerleaders, cartoons on the displays – and how relaxed people were – Americans would never think to have a picnic at a professional baseball game.

Koreans traveling to the USA, Canada or UK have similar opportunities to discover new and interesting cultural activities. We chose the activities below because they are common and very different from what you can experience in Korea.

From left to right - American man stands outside his offroad-modified truck on a difficult dirt road. A British man does "mud bogging," where he attempts to drive his truck through deep mud. A man in a modified Jeep does "rock crawling." A custom built offroad truck drives over old vans.

Off-roading is a group of sports common in the US, Great Britain and Canada. People buy and modify 4x4 trucks in order to drive on extreme terrain. Types of off-roading include mud bogging, rock crawling and trail driving. Off-roading is most popular among rural people and it's not just for men. Almost half of off-roaders are women! Remember, in the US, Canada and in Great Britain, many rich people live in rural areas. As such, you will see many very, very expensive off-road trucks.

Rodeo is most common in the USA and Canada. These are sports that come from cowboys and including bull riding, bronco busting and roping. Cowboys and cowgirls demonstrate their skills catching and training farm animals. Some rodeo sports are very dangerous and most of them are very exciting. Koreans visiting the US or Canada will certainly have a unique experience if they visit a rodeo.

From left to right - A woman races her horse at a Canadian rodeo. A cowboy competes in bull riding. Another cowboy uses a rope to catch a calf, an event called "calf roping," at a Canadian rodeo. A young boy attempts to ride a sheep, called "mutton busting," at a rodeo in the USA.

Dating is different in the US, UK and Canada than in Korea. In Korea, couples usually don't kiss in public or even hug. In the USA, Canada or UK, it is a little bit strange if a girlfriend and boyfriend don't kiss when they say goodbye. Further, asking someone out in the US, UK or Canada is usually much less complicated than in Korea. If an American man likes a new woman, he will simply say "I like you, let's get coffee." Likewise, if a British woman likes a man, she can say "you should ask me out." Rejections are common, but they are not usually treated as shameful. Anglo-Americans often "split the bill" or "Dutch pay," meaning each person pays for half of the cost of the date.

From left to right - American actors and couple Ashton Kutcher and Demi Moore hold hands in public. An older couple kisses in public

From left to right - This potluck party is in an American church. Guests all bring homemade food and share with their friends. Friends in Colorado (USA) gather at a house party.

Parties are potentially very interesting for Koreans visiting Britain, the USA or Canada. Anglo-Americans often have house parties and potluck parties. The host will provide some food and alcohol, but the guests will bring most of the snacks. There will often be music in the house along with games and BBQ. Parties in bars, like is common in Korea, are less common in the USA, Canada and Britain. Also, different from Korea, people in bars do not have to order food (안주).

From left to right - Fans of the Oakland Raiders at an American football game. Chelsea (UK) celebrating a soccer championship with a parade. Several thousand fans celebrating before a hockey championship game.

If Korean people visit the UK in particular, they will notice that sports fans are very intense. Soccer games between two cities will be the biggest events of the week. People paint their faces, decorate their cars and wear special jerseys to support their teams. In the US, the biggest sport is American Football. Contrary to what many Koreans think, American football is one of the most strategically complicated games in the world – think of it as violent chess. In Canada, the main sport is ice hockey, which millions of Canadians play on the weekends.

From left to right - British man hunts foxes with the help of blood hounds. Man preparing to hunt (probably birds) with a bow. American man poses with the deer he killed. Hunters usually eat the animals they kill and use the skins to make clothes.

In contrast with Korea, guns are legal in Canada, the USA and, to a lesser extent, the UK. As such, all three countries have rich traditions of hunting. In the USA and Canada, people can hunt deer, antelope, wild goats and even bears. In the UK, the most common animals to hunt are birds and foxes. People in all three countries are usually good at gun safety and hunting is not particularly dangerous to the hunters.

From left to right – Ben Garrido, one author of this book, cutting old metal to make a car part. Handmade house in California (USA). Magazine teaching people how to make a radio

Anglo-Americans love to build things by hand. People enjoy making everything from furniture to gardens to entire houses. People build radios in their front rooms, computers in their garages and special, classic tuner cars in their yards. Because of this, Americans have enormous stores, like the Home Depot, that sell nothing but Do It Yourself (DIY) products. Koreans visiting Britain, Canada or the USA have a great opportunity to learn DIY skills in hundreds of popular categories.

#1

In your opinion, which cultural activity seems most enjoyable?

#2

Which activities do you think are exciting and which ones do you feel uncomfortable about?

Exciting	Uncomfortable
1. 2.	1. 2.

#3

Which activities do you think would be popular in Korea? Explain your reasons.

Final Word:

We hope you've enjoyed this book and encourage both teachers and students to pursue outside research on all of these stories. The individuals and events in this textbook all merit further study. If you'd like to peruse more works by Young-Joo Jeon, you can find more articles at Daejeon Ilbo and www.riss4u. If you'd like to check out Ben Garrido's other works, "The Blackguard" is available at www.bengarrido.com/buy-ben-garridos-books, "Critical Thinking for Leaders" is available through Shinasa Publishing company and hundreds of free-to-use essays are available at www.bengarrido.com.

The authors would like to thank Seung-hwee Oh and Do-su Lee for their excellent editing and sage advice on the fine points of Korean culture. We would further like to recognize Harold Kim for translating some of the trickier sections into Korean, Chris Marsh and Tom Cecil for helping us with specifically British and Canadian sections. Garret Hohn endured the tedium of graphics and layout design. Further, we would like to thank Yoon-mi Jung for many valuable contributions to the questions and activities sections in each chapter.

Finally, the authors would like to specially recognize the contributions of Professor Park Chur-woong. Professor Park volunteered several months of his time helping us analyze, improve and expand these chapters. His help was invaluable and we're not sure the book would not exist in its current form without his contributions.

Author Information:

Ben Garrido is the author of the novels The Blackguard and The Potency (available soon). He also writes award winning journalism for the Reno News and Review, Chico News and Review and others, and lectures on second language acquisition at Mokwon University in South Korea. His other textbook, also published by Shinasa, is "Origins of Anglo-American Culture." He writes on subjects including language, fiction, adventure and logic on his website, www.bengarrido.com. Raised in Reno, Nevada, he now divides his time between South Korea and the United States.

Young-Joo Jeon has a Ph. D in English education and has been a professor of English education department at Mokwon University. She had taught English in several middle and high schools for 15 years before. She has been involved in many different government projects in English education policy, teaching methodology and classroom observation. She has published books on classroom English and high-school English textbooks. She has published many articles in the area of primary & secondary school English education, and classroom observation & analysis and so on.

Anglo-American Culture

First Published Aug 21. 2017
SHINASA Publishing Co.
4, Tongil-ro 59-gil, Eunpyeong-gu, Seoul, Korea
Registered : 9-52 (Jan. 5 1956)
Tel: 02-382-6411
Fax: 02-382-6401
E-mail: shinasa@hanmail.net
Homepage: www.shinasa.co.kr

ISBN : 978-89-8396-235-5(93740)
Printed and bounded in Korea

₩ 15000